DUBLIN

DUBLIN

Brian Solomon

CHARTWELL
BOOKS, INC.

To all the Gunns of John Gunn
Camera—Wexford Street, Dublin

This edition published in 2008 by

CHARTWELL BOOKS, INC.
A Division of
BOOK SALES, INC.
114 Northfield Avenue
Edison, New Jersey 08837

ISBN-13: 978-0-7858-2472-5
ISBN-10: 0-7858-2472-3

Cataloging-in-Publication data is available from the Library of Congress

Design: Ian Hughes/Compendium Design

Photography: All images are by Brian Solomon, except pages 54 and 66 by Maureen Solomon

Printed and bound in China

Page 1: A close-up of a street light on Merrion Street Upper reveals the cleverly placed shamrock in the decorative iron work.

Page 2-3: The effect of the "Celtic Tiger" has Dublin bustling with commerce and awash in colorful lights—arches of the Grattan Bridge are lit from below with green flood lamps.

Right: The quayside buildings at Arran Quay reflect in the unusually placid waters of the Liffey. Today the river is tidal as far as Islandbridge; the water level rises and falls several feet during the course of the day.

Contents

TO LET
RESERVED
KILBRIDE

Acknowledgments

Over the last decade, I've enjoyed a great many hours exploring Dublin's streets and alleys—as well as its pubs, museums, architectural wonders, bridges and railway lines—while tracing its history, taking photographs and perusing the literature of the city. Much of this was accomplished through the help of many friends who led the way, suggested itineraries, accompanied me during photographic and walking tours, as well as visits to Dublin's innumerable pubs.

Thanks to everyone, including: Tessa Bold; Anthony "Booster" Bools; Barry and David Carse; John Cleary; Diarmaid and Gearoid Collins; Anne Condon; Katherine Condon; Phil and Sarah Cox; Paul and Sarah Dowd; Ken Fox; Rob Fisher; Heike Fauter; Cathy and Fiona Gunn; Mick Guilfoyle; Mark Healy; David Hegarty; Stephen Hirsch; Mark Hodge; Colin Malachy; Peter Matthews; Denis McCabe; Norman McAdams; Gerry Mooney; Dave Murphy; Colm O'Callighan; Diane O'Connell; Hassard Stacpoole; and to my brother Seán Solomon.

Colin Horan helped with detailed inspections of the city center and proofread drafts of the text. Special thanks to the Irish Railway Record Society for the use of their library and answers to innumerable questions. Thanks to IRRS members: Brian and Niall Torpey for stepping me through engineering details of Dublin Port and bridge engineering; Tim Moriarty for details on the Irish language, Dublin history and particulars on Irish railways; Seamas Ratigan for detailed overviews of Dublin architecture, history and politics; and Peter Rigney for help with place names. Thanks also to everyone involved in the Railway Preservation Society for spins on their historic trains and details of Dublin's railway history. Thanks to Irish Rail's Heritage Officer Gregg Ryan for a tour of the Inchicore Works.

Dublin's essential fabric is more than just its architecture, geography and history—it includes its rich and complex culture. Dublin's taxi drivers have been a great help, not only delivering me to my destinations but helping me sort through literary and history problems at all hours of the day and night. Famous for its writers, Dublin has been chronicled in some of the richest literature of the English language and, with this body of work, many of the city's mysteries have been unraveled, and an equal number created. Contemporary culture has produced a great array of radio, film and other types of modern media. I've been a regular listener to Today FM, finding it a great source of music, media, propaganda, news and weather reports. The Gallery of Photography at Meeting House Square provided crucial photographic support in my early years in Dublin. Photo Care on Abbey Street provided color film and color slide processing while everyone at Gunn's Camera on Wexford Street took a special interest in my photography, providing me with suggestions, film and contacts. My parents, Maureen and Richard Solomon, have visited me in Ireland and took time to review photographs and text. Thanks to Simon Forty at Compendium Publishing for helping make boxes of photos and an idea into this book. I've made every effort to keep my text accurate, honest and informative...if any errors appear they are my own.

PREVIOUS PAGE: This evening view of the River Liffey shows the Grattan Bridge and Ormond Quay. In the seventeenth century, the Duke of Ormond's vision of Dublin had been inspired by recent quayside development along the Seine in Paris.

FOLLOWING PAGE: Custom House on the River Liffey—see page 23. *The Image Bank/ Macduff Everton/Getty Images*

RIGHT: Quintessential Dublin—Ha'Penny Bridge, the River Liffey, a handsome Georgian terrace, and sunshine. Dublin has a total average annual rainfall of 762mm which is less than Dallas or New York.

PIERSE

Introduction

For many years, Dublin was characterized by its glorious decay. Prosperity has now swept over the city, transforming it in ways unimaginable just a few decades ago. In some ways, central Dublin is recognizable as the city of James Joyce; in others it seems to be a cosmopolitan menagerie that has little to do with the dirty old town of years gone by. Long a tear-stained port for emigrants, Dublin has enjoyed and absorbed an unprecedented influx of immigrants—both returning Irish from abroad, as well as people from nations around the world. Today's Dublin is filled with thriving African, Asian, eastern European and Middle Eastern communities—people who have brought with them food, culture, music, attire and skills to add to Dublin's ever more eclectic tapestry of life. It has been repeated so often as to be a cliché, but one is more likely to hear Mandarin spoken in Dublin than any dialect of native Irish (except when riding the new tram system called the LUAS, as announcements are given in Irish and English).

Dublin has grown at a furious pace. While there has been much new construction around the traditional center, this pales in comparison to the suburban growth which has raced outward. At the height of its boom, Dublin appeared to change on a daily basis with new buildings sprouting like fungi after rain. In a passing glance, the field once filled with grazing sheep is now spotted with new houses instead. Much of the new development, especially that in the suburbs, lacks the style, character and history of the architecture that has typified Georgian and Victorian Dublin. There is no mistaking Dublin's new growth for that of yesteryear.

Dublin is a dynamic city of contrasts and a complex historical place that grasps at modernity. To understand Dublin, one needs to appreciate its history. Although impossible to ignore, the history of Dublin is difficult to comprehend. Yet, its own denizens live in an odd mixture of historical embrace and ambivalence. One cannot go anywhere in the city center without being thrust into Dublin's multifaceted history. It seems that hardly a building is without a plaque, a footpath without a marker, or a traffic island without a monument to someone intrinsic to Dublin's past. At the same time, seemingly incongruous monoliths of modernity have been erected that pose an awkward contrast with their historical surroundings—to purists, it is blasphemy; to admirers of dynamic growth, it is bliss; to most, it is something in between.

The novice tourist may be captivated by the Georgian splendor, the youthful vibe and the cosmopolitan infusion, while the lifelong resident is merely troubled by traffic gridlock, Dublin's rocketing prices and, perhaps, nostalgia for the way things were before the "Celtic Tiger"...the wave of prosperity that has swept the city in recent years. Those same things that have made Dublin great, can also be attributed to its imperfections.

Too often the dynamics of Dublin's and Ireland's history have been misrepresented in polarized terms—Irish versus English; Protestant versus Catholic; "Culchie" versus "Jackeen"; North-sider versus South-sider—such clear delineations tend to be over simplifications that neither represent, nor explain, the real complexities at hand. The mindset of the "Eighteenth Century Ascendancy" and how that affected the location of the Customs House isn't really all that important today. The good and the bad; the visionary and the inept; and the well-meaning and the self-serving have all contributed to modern Dublin.

Dublin was a Viking city, yet today the only Viking presence one is likely to see today are Nouveaux-Vikings marauding about in amphibious tour boats, or those lining the streets on St. Patrick's Day adorned in furry Viking helmets dyed in the Tri-Color. Likewise, the Dublin of Anglo-Norman times was largely erased centuries ago with just a few vestiges visible to the closely discerning tourist. Yet, the Vikings put Dublin on the European map and the Anglo-Normans gave Dublin its castle, around which the city developed and grew. Today, the stylized castle remains a symbol of the city. But the real castle, much altered from its twelfth century form, no longer plays a central role in the average Dubliner's daily life. Dublin's city center, and the streets and buildings radiating to the rough circle circumscribed by the canals, are largely the result of Georgian planning and architects and it is a tone that defines central Dublin. The Victorians spread Dublin into the suburbs, connected outlying areas with new roads, railway lines and trams, and blessed the city center with numerous impressive buildings, including many of its great pubs.

In the twentieth century, Ireland's independence produced a great many changes: new buildings; further suburban development; and re-naming of streets, bridges and institutions. The lost tourist looking for Kingsbridge Station will find little help from modern maps, yet it still lies only a short distance away within sight of the Wellington Testimonial in the Phoenix Park.

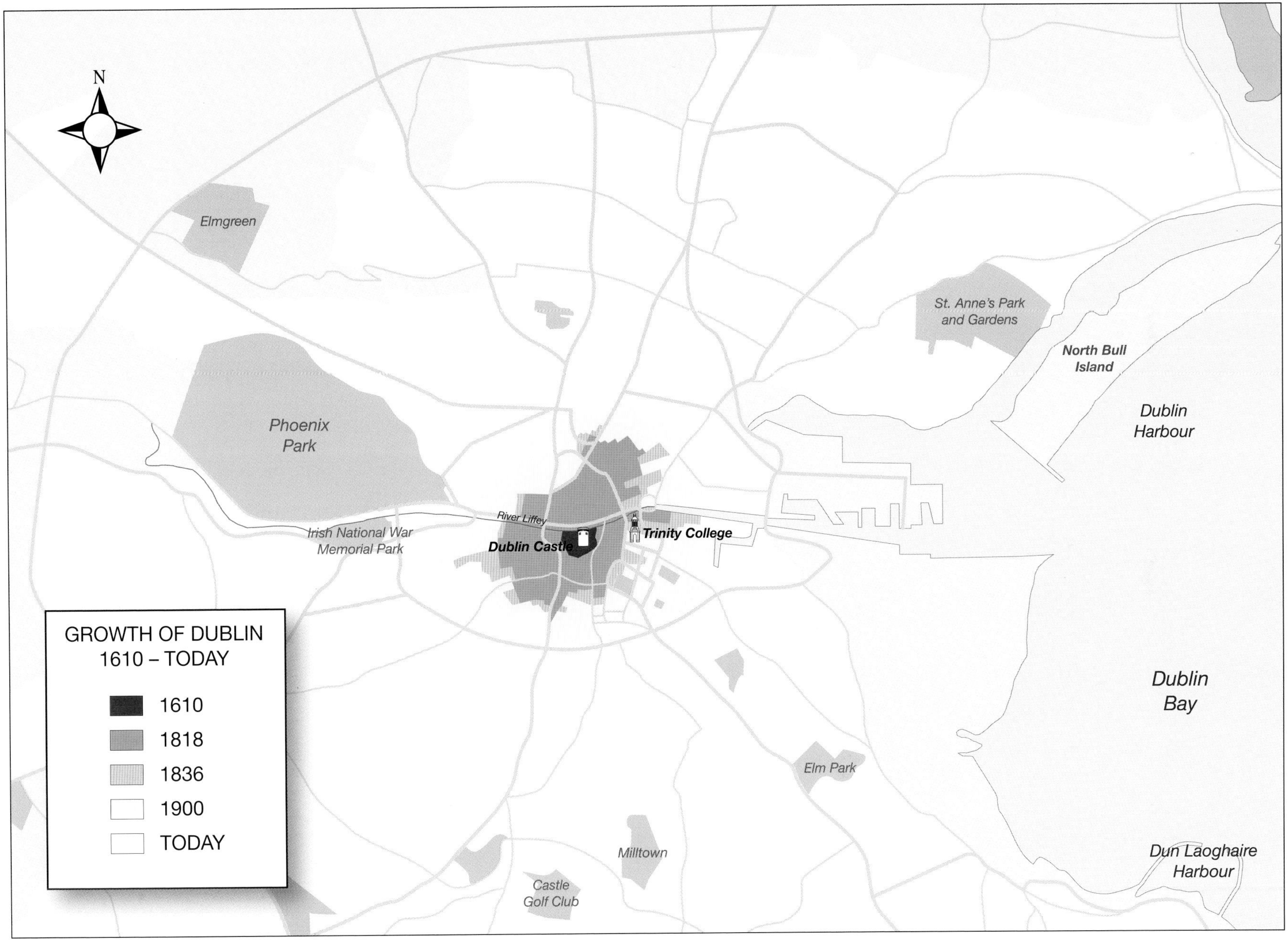
N
Elmgreen
St. Anne's Park
and Gardens
North Bull
Island
Dublin
Harbour
Phoenix
Park
River Liffey
Irish National War
Memorial Park
Dublin Castle
Trinity College
Dublin
Bay
Elm Park
Milltown
Castle
Golf Club
Dun Laoghaire
Harbour
GROWTH OF DUBLIN
1610 – TODAY
1610
1818
1836
1900
TODAY

FAR LEFT: Buildings along Arran Quay catch the morning sun. The clock tower on the right belongs to St. Paul's Church at Smithfield.

LEFT: The Merchants' Arch covers a footpath that leads from Temple Bar to the Ha'Penny footbridge, giving pedestrians direct access to the north side shopping areas. The arch dates to 1821, and is credited to Frederick Darley, architect of the Merchants' Building.

RIGHT: Dublin Bus uses a stylized castle as its herald. Many of the city center bus routes still follow lines established by electric street trams in the Victorian era.

FAR RIGHT: Image versus reality: a seasonal ad for Guinness stout hangs from the walls of a rotting abandoned building along the Liffey quays only a short distance from the brewery.

BUS
O'Connell

3782/8886
More O'Ferrall
CHRISTMAS IS ANTICIPATION
GUINNES
Enjoy GUINNESS Sensibly

LEFT: The main entrance to Trinity College faces College Green. Although the college dates from 1592, most of its prominent buildings were designed in Georgian times. This portal gateway was constructed in the 1750s.

RIGHT: A statue of Jesus on O'Connell Street basks in the sun on Christmas morning 2007.

THE bagel BAR
THE bagel BAR
Top Class Alterations
JO
PARIS
EXCEPT
TRAMS
AND ACCESS
INTERNET CALL SHOP
KIELY'S

Left: A LUAS trams rolls down Middle Abbey Street on a rainy evening.

BUS
GUESTHOUSE
THE CHARLES STEWART
BED & BREAKFAST

Left: Parnell Square's magnificent terraced houses echo the vision of Dublin's eighteenth century planners whose imprint can be seen all over the city center.

Right: Dublin's symbolism can be found in the details of the city's infrastructure. The ever-present castle harks back to Dublin's Norman past.

LEFT: St. Patrick's Day is a national holiday. Many Irish go all out, wrapping themselves in the Tri-Color and dressing as leprechauns as a matter of national pride.

RIGHT: Dublin's Custom House catches a ray of sun as thick cloud races across the sky. Considered by many the masterwork of English architect James Gandon, the Custom House is well executed in the neo-Classical style that typified public buildings of the Georgian period.

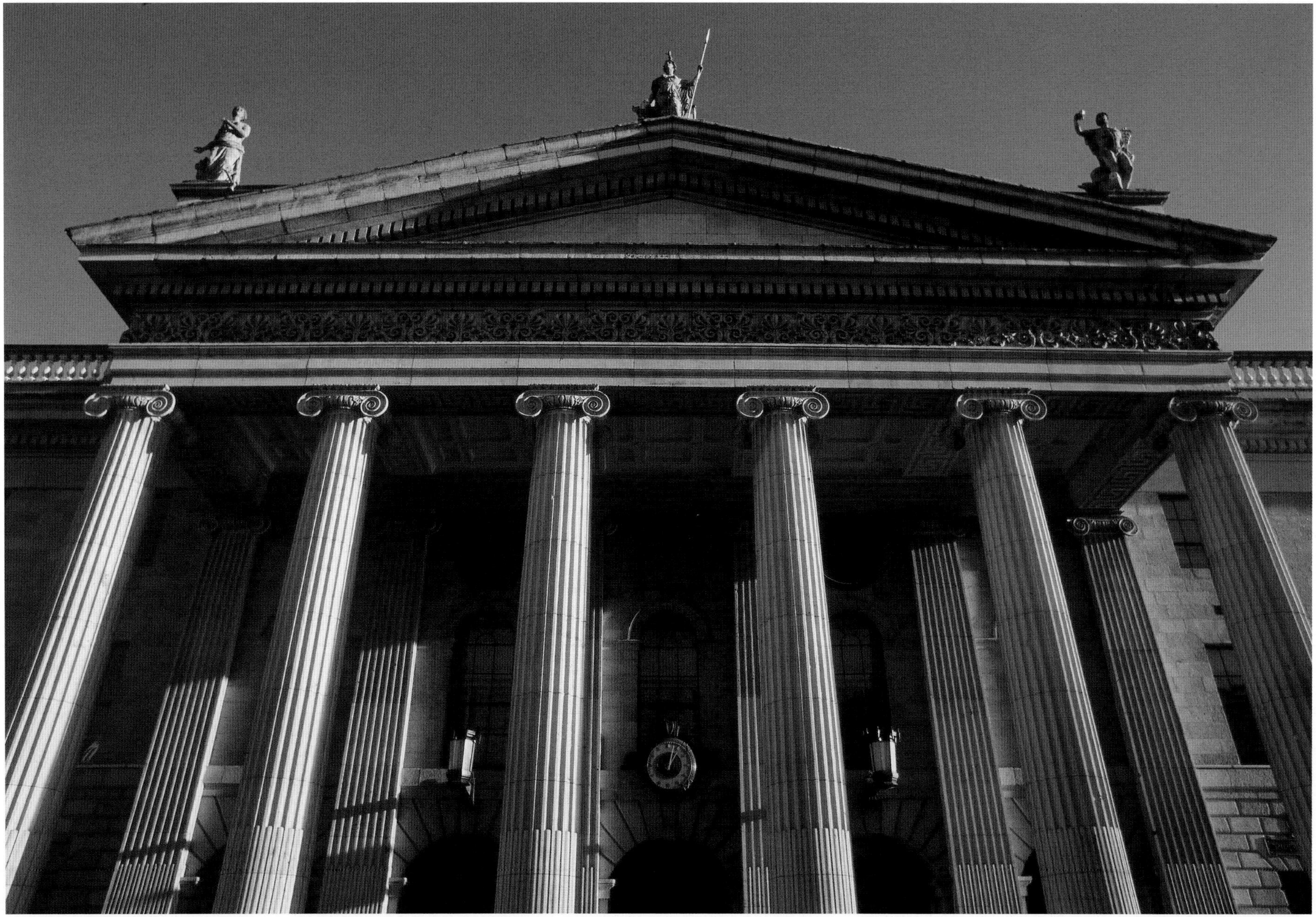

LEFT: Completed in 1818, Dublin's General Post Office was designed by Francis Johnson who carried on the aesthetic for public buildings that had been established in the eighteenth century. GPO's role in the 1916 Rising made it a symbol of Irish independence.

RIGHT: Dublin's urban environs have long fascinated artists, architects and writers.

RIGHT: O'Connell Street stretches away behind the statue of Daniel O'Connell by John Foley. Batchelor's Walk at left; Eden Quay at right; and the O'Connell Bridge in the foreground. *IIC/Axiom/Getty Images*

IRISH NATIONWIDE BUILDING SOCIETY
NO ENTRY
NO ENTRY

FAR LEFT: With arms thrust in the air, the statue of trade union leader Jim Larken on O'Connell Street captures the pose of his rousing speech in 1913. He spoke from a balcony in the Imperial Hotel (Clery's department store) on the east side of the street opposite the statue.

LEFT: The base of this old cast iron street lamp has recently been improved by the coloring of Dublin's coat of arms.

RIGHT: St. Joseph's Church's impressive stone façade.

FAR RIGHT: Framed in the railing posts of the Mellowes Bridge, buildings along Dublin's Arran Quay catch the morning sun. At the center is the clock tower of St. Paul's Church at Smithfield.

FOLLOWING PAGE: The Liffey is swollen with the rising tide. In Viking times, the river looked very different with expanses of shallow water on both sides of the main channel.

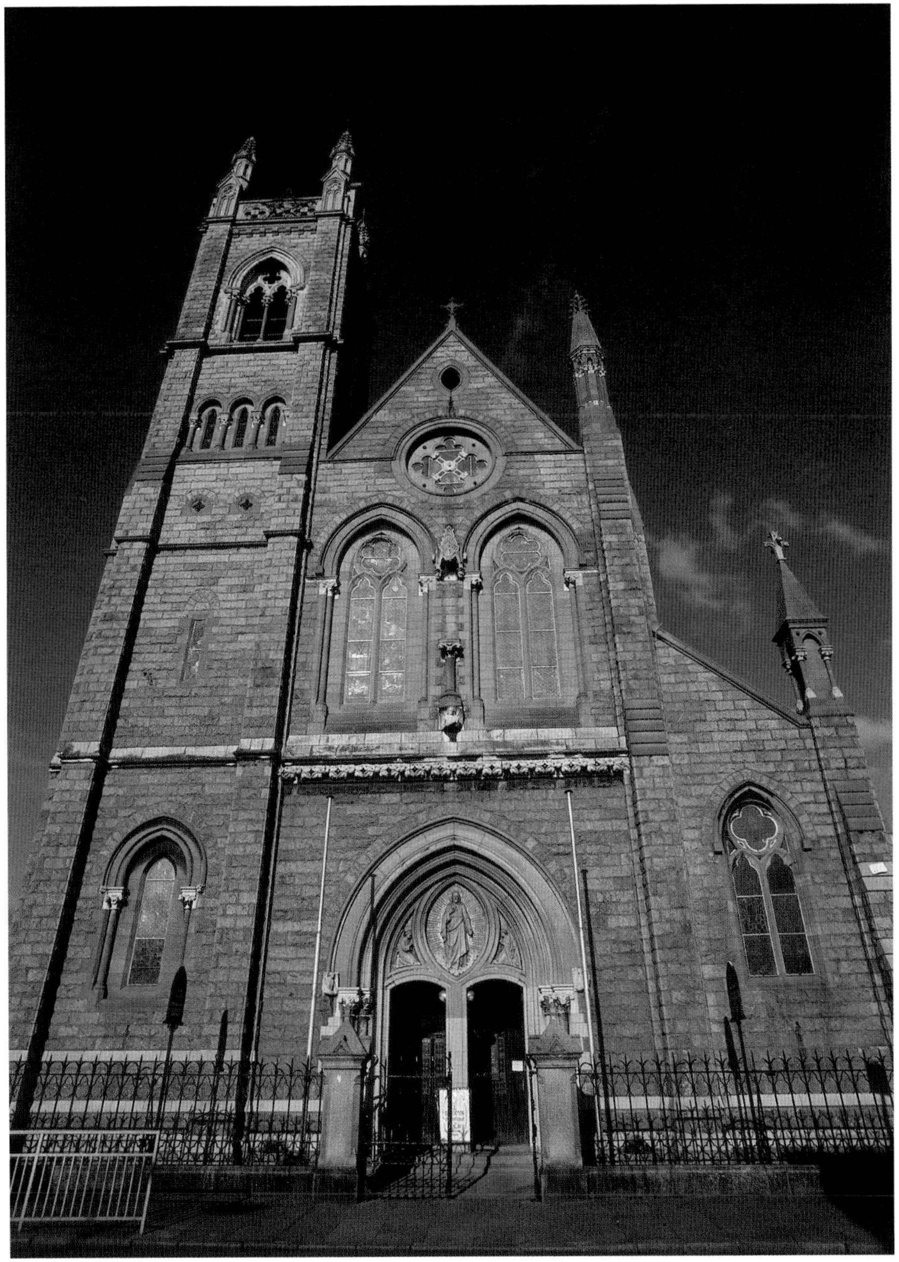

INN ON THE LIFFEY

The Phoenix Park
Tea Rooms

LEFT: The Phoenix Park Tea Room retains its Victorian elegance.

RIGHT: Ancient Dublin.

COFFEE

LEFT: Layers of Dublin: pedestrians cross the Millennium and Ha'Penny (Liffey) footbridges. Beyond, buses roll over O'Connell Bridge, an Irish Rail train crosses the elevated Liffey Viaduct on Loop Line of 1891, all against a backdrop of the Custom House and the modern International Financial Services Center.

RIGHT: Ornamental shamrocks adorn the iron railings in front of the National Gallery on Merrion Square.

FOLLOWING PAGE: The Millennium Bridge was installed over the River Liffey in 1999 and opened as part of Dublin's year 2000 rehab. Unlike the much older and more famous Liffey foot bridge, this modern bridge bounces noticeably under the weight of pedestrians.

TEMPLE BAR
GALLERY
STUDIOS

ELIZA LODGE
RESTAURANT
FITZ IMONS HOTEL

Early Dublin

Early Dublin

Ecclesiastical settlement, Vikings and Normans

Ireland has been home to civilized peoples for at least eight millennia. It is the location of some of the world's best-preserved early human construction. The tomb at Newgrange and nearby sites north of Dublin rank as some of the oldest man-made enclosures in the world, predating the first pyramids in Egypt by hundreds of years. Yet very little is known about early settlement in Dublin, and much of what we accept is based on archaeology, scant mentions in old literature and educated speculation rather than documented history.

The banks of the River Liffey in the vicinity of today's Dublin hosted various prehistoric settlements. Later it was known for early ecclesiastical settlements, then Viking, followed by Anglo-Norman conquerors. Despite the large number of ruins and well-preserved sites elsewhere in Ireland, precious little can be seen in today's Dublin that is more than five centuries old. Shrouded in the mists of time, early Dublin may be appreciated through stories, recollections and myths, and through vestiges of early buildings, as well as artifacts displayed at the National Museum on Kildare Street.

Physical evidence of Ireland's earliest peoples indicates that Celtic tribes settled during the fourth and fifth centuries BC, and surely displaced or intermarried with earlier peoples. Celtic ballads and literature have survived to hint at what these people were like. Unlike classical European civilizations in Greece or Rome, neither the Celts—nor the peoples that preceded them—built substantial cities. Any structures they erected were largely built of wood. Outside Dublin some stone structures exist, but nothing along the lines of ancient cities in Egypt, Greece or Italy.

The Celts certainly had some settlement at Dublin. Viking descriptions lead us to believe there were prehistoric burial grounds in the vicinity of what is now College Green in the city center. The Vikings called this Hoggen Green—"hogges" was Norse for a mound, presumably similar to ancient burial mounds still found elsewhere in Ireland.

The defining elements of prehistoric Dublin were an important crossroads west of today's Christ Church, religious structures and a crude Liffey crossing probably near the present-day Father Mathew Bridge which led to the crossroads. This crossing was known in Irish as the "Átha Cliath", loosely translated as "ford of hurdles" or "(a) ford of sticks"; the surrounding settlement known therefore as "Baile Átha Cliath" ("The town of Ford of the Hurdles") and this remains today as the Irish name for Dublin.

St. Patrick is understood to have founded a church in Ireland near the site of the cathedral, built hundreds of years later, that bears his name. Today a stone marker identifies the location of St. Patrick's well, purportedly used by him to baptize converts to the Christian faith. Whether St. Patrick actually visited Dublin is not certain, but church settlements developed at several locations on the south banks of the Liffey and it is quite likely that a more substantial community was also in place at the time.

As early as the late eighth century, Vikings or Norsemen are known to have made raids on the Irish coast. More significant were planned invasions about 831–832 AD that resulted in permanent settlement in Ireland, with a Viking town established along the Liffey by 840. In those times, people had little warning of such attacks: imagine the trepidation and foreboding a cautiously observing monk or friar must have felt on that unrecorded rainy morning in the ninth century when the first Viking longboat oared up the Liffey. Little could he have known, nor probably cared, that this ship (or ships) was the seed that would grow into Ireland's foremost metropolis.

A large vertical stone was planted near where that first ship was anchored. Known as a Steine (sometimes spelled Steyne), this was located near the present day junction of Pearse, Fleet, D'Olier and College Streets north of Trinity College, where the River Steyne flowed into the Liffey. The Viking Long Stone stood for the better part of nine hundred years until it was removed during expansion of the city in the 1720s. However, in the mid-1980s, the Steine Monument was reinstalled to mark the approximate spot of the original stone. Not far away is a pub, The Long Stone, where one can enjoy a bowl of soup and a pint.

For nearly two centuries, the Vikings lived along the Liffey and developed a significant community. Over time, they intermarried with Celtic Irish while adopting Irish habits, culture and language. Dublin, however, looked nothing like it does today. The river was more sinuous, two to three times wider, and fed by clearly visible tributaries such as the Poddle which flowed into the Liffey near the west end of today's Dame Street. Above this confluence was a pond known for its inky

Previous page: St. Patrick's Cathedral was founded in 1191. *IIC/Axiom/Getty Images*

Right: Dublin's Christ Church cathedral occupies the site of an earlier eleventh century wooden church established by Irish-Viking king Sigtryggr (Sitric) Silkbeard.

complexion that was a preferred Viking berthing point known to historians as a "Longphort". To the Irish, this location was "Dubh Linn", (some times spelled Duibhlinne) meaning "black pool". To the Vikings this was "Dyflin", and undoubtedly the pronunciation would sound foreign to today's ears. Centuries ago, this was anglicized as "Dubline" and finally Dublin. In those times "Dubh Linn" was likely treated as a distinct place from "Átha Cliath". Ironically, the most enduring element of the Vikings' settlement was attaching the name of this pond to the city. Most other traces of Viking Dublin have been erased by later denizens.

It is difficult to imagine how the city appeared in Viking times. Excavations have revealed remains of various primitive wooden structures. The local Viking government is understood to have convened on a small hillock, known as the Thingmote (or *Thingmount)*, roughly the location of today's Dublin tourist office—formerly the Church of St. Andrews, on the street of the same name. Of the Thingmote nothing remains because the hillock was used as landfill along nearby Nassau Street, then prone to flooding, around 1685.

The Vikings constructed longboats in Dublin, using the city as a base for raids elsewhere in Ireland and across the Irish Sea to Britain. Soon their settlement spread up the hill to the defensible high ground where Christ Church is now located. They also had a settlement about two miles west in the vicinity of today's Islandbridge and Kilmainham.

Relations with the Irish were tumultuous. The Vikings were rousted from Dublin around 897 by a local Irish chieftain, but they reclaimed the city less than a generation later. Then in the eleventh century, Irish clans—led by Brian Boru, the King of Munster—fought a series of wars to rid Ireland of Viking domination. The climax of this campaign occurred in 1014 when the forces of Boru

LEFT: On a frosty morning, the sun glints off the O'Donovan Rossa Bridge and Winetavern Street looking toward the Dublin City Council offices and beyond to the Christ Church cathedral.

defeated the Vikings at the River Tolka in Clontarf (now part of Dublin's north side). This marked the end of Viking supremacy in Ireland and, from that point onward, the remaining Norsemen were politically and socially integrated in Irish life. These tamed Irish Vikings are known as Hiberno-Norse and over time had more in common with the Irish then their traditional ancestors. Significantly, they adopted Christianity. In 1038, Hiberno-Norse Viking king Silkbeard organized the construction of a wooden Christian church on the site of what later developed into Christ Church cathedral. Hiberno-Norse Dublin grew as an important European trading center as craftsmen and small industries flourished.

The Seat of Anglo-Norman Power

Despite the neutralizing Norse influence, Irish clans of the eleventh and twelfth centuries were anything but cohesive. In the mid-twelfth century, a power struggle between Irish clans resulted in an inopportune invitation to Anglo-Norman King Henry II to send troops to Ireland. They arrived under the leadership of Strongbow and established an Anglo-Norman powerbase in Dublin at the time of its capture in 1171. Henry linked Dublin politically with Normans in Bristol which ended Dublin's independence and paved the way for gradual Norman conquest of Ireland. Clashes and co-operation between Anglo-Norman conquerors and the native Irish resulted in a difficult and multifaceted history that inextricably linked Irish and British chronology.

Over the ensuing centuries, a complex, tumultuous and often violent relationship evolved in Ireland between the ruling classes and native peoples. Nevertheless, as a result of the Anglo-Norman invasion, Dublin emerged as their foremost stronghold in Ireland and flourished as the seat of power, learning and trade. The story goes that the Hiberno-

Right: Detail of Christ Church; although the essential structure of the cathedral is Medieval, its present appearance is largely the result of the 1870s restoration by George Edmund Street.

Norse left established Dublin for new settlements on the north side of the Liffey known as Oxmantown. There were already significant religious sites in place on the north side. Of greatest interest are St. Mary's Cistercian Abbey—dissolved in 1539 which lends its name to present day Abbey Street (the old chapter house still stands)—and St. Michan's Church, portions of which are not only extant but still serve as a church. During the thirteenth century, the old ford was replaced by a stone bridge. With the Anglo-Normans came a much clearer view of Dublin's history as result of surviving records from their administrative bureaucracy and other written accounts.

The Anglo-Norman powerbase was Dublin Castle, constructed between 1204 and 1228 near or on the location of the black pool. Around this a Medieval walled city was built. The River Poddle was diverted to flow around three sides of the castle and city to serve as a protective moat—difficult to visualize today, since the Poddle was channeled underground between the seventeenth and nineteenth centuries and there is little evidence of it today in the city center.

One of the city walls ran along modern day Ship Street, where a portion of the old stones can still be seen. More obvious is the remaining portions of the old wall along Cook Street—so named because this was where cooking fires were made beyond the walls. The other walls are long gone but, in recent times, historic markers have been placed on city streets that show the position of the wall. Entry to the walled city was gained via several strategically placed city gates. St. Audoen's Gate, near the medieval church of the same name, survives on the northwest side of the old city off Cook Street. Another gate is remembered by the street named Wormwood Gate.

The area around Dublin was fortified and secure. The ruling classes within the city walls and in the greater city knew it as "the Pale". They viewed this as a civilized refuge beyond which was a strange and hostile country. Gradually, as Ireland was further settled by Anglo-Norman/British people, "the Pale" was extended beyond Dublin. The city walls lost their strategic significance as the city spread well beyond their confines.

Medieval Dublin was a maze of narrow winding lanes, both inside and beyond the wall. Although few medieval buildings have survived, much of street layout in the vicinity of the old city can trace roots to these medieval lanes, some of which dated to Viking times. One of the oldest is Fishamble Street, located just east of Christ Church, and named for the fish market held there. Likewise Cornmarket Street earned its name from its location of a medieval corn market.

The most important structure outside the wall on the south side was St. Patrick's Cathedral, founded in 1171 on the site of an existing church (its distinctive tower dates to 1362). The church was strategically situated near the confluence of the Coombe stream and the Poddle which provided an element of protection. (The winding street called The Coombe evolved from an ancient road that followed the stream. As with other Dublin waterways, the stream was channeled underground centuries ago.) Although everything around the Cathedral has changed, portions of the old structure remain.

St. Patrick's most famous dean was Jonathan Swift, better known today for his writings (amongst them *Gulliver's Travels*) and discussions of the plight of the poor

living in the areas known as the "Liberties" to the southwest of the old walls. By the nineteenth century, St. Patrick's had become a ruin and was largely rebuilt with money provided by Lord Iveagh—Sir Benjamin Lee Guinness, descendant of Arthur Guinness, founder of the nearby Guinness brewery.

Inside the wall is Dublin's other cathedral, Christ Church, possibly among the first buildings to be improved by the Normans. The crypt dates to 1172 and is often cited as the oldest surviving structure in Dublin. Interred there are the remains of Strongbow, Dublin's first Anglo-Norman ruler. The church was modified over the centuries but, like St. Patrick's, suffered from neglect; the building standing today is largely the result of Victorian-era remodeling. The foundations of the twelfth century chapter house have been exposed in front of the present church.

The eastern-most entry to the old city was at Dame Gate, near the site of the old St. Mary del Dam church—named for the dam on the Poddle possibly dating from early Norman times. From this gate was a pathway that extended toward the Augustine Priory that once stood on the site now occupied by Trinity College. Over the years, this path developed into one of Dublin's principal thoroughfares, Dame Street. The importance of this street grew after the establishment of Trinity College by Queen Elizabeth I in 1592.

BELOW LEFT: St. Patrick's Minot Tower and St. Patrick's Cathedral. Dublin has grown and evolved around this seven hundred year old structure that once sat on an island in the River Poddle. *iStockphoto*

BELOW: Dublin's "Liberties" at the corner of Dean Street and New Row. Three hundred years ago, this was one of Dublin's poorest neighborhoods.

LEFT: While it is probable that this effigy is not one of Richard fitz Gilbert de Clare, Earl of Pembroke—"Strongbow"— he was certainly buried in Christ Church Cathedral. He had come to Ireland at the invitation of Dermot MacMurchada, king of Leinster. Dermot offered Strongbow his daughter Eve (Aoife) in marriage as well as the kingdom of Leinster on Dermot's death, if Strongbow helped Dermot regain his kingdom. After Dermot died at Ferns in May 1171, Strongbow assumed the kingship of Leinster in right of his wife. Strongbow died in June 1176 and was buried with great ceremony.

FAR LEFT: In the crypt of Christ Church Cathedral, Dublin. Commissioned by the Norman conqueror of Dublin in 1172, the church fell into a poor state of repair by the 19th century and had to be remodeled in the 1870s by architect George Street. Monuments removed during the restoration are on show in the crypt today.

Left: Medieval Dublin developed around an Anglo-Norman garrison and was protected by city walls.

Right: The remnants of the old city wall along Cook Street gives a sense of how medieval Dublin may have appeared. Most of the walls were demolished centuries ago.

LEFT: Dublin's only surviving medieval gate is this portal at St. Audoen's Gate which leads to the church of the same name. By the early seventeenth century, two thirds of Dublin residents were living beyond the old walls.

RIGHT: The castle has been Dublin's coat of arms for some seven hundred years.

ATA

FAR LEFT: The Lord Edward is a pub on Werburgh Street near Christ Church. It is named for Lord Edward Fitzgerald, one of the United Irishmen martyred in the 1798 Rebellion.

LEFT: A Christmas poster for Dublin plays on symbols of the city's history.

RIGHT: The Steyne (Steine) Monument is a 1980s creation marking the approximate location of the ninth century Viking marker that stood until the 1720s.

FAR RIGHT: Dubliners are out in numbers for the annual St. Patrick's Day parade, seen here across the street from the medieval cathedral named after Ireland's patron saint.

RIGHT: Enthusiastic young Vikings clamber for a view of floats in the 2008 St. Patrick's Day parade.

FAR RIGHT: Today, the glass encased offices of Dublin City Council (formerly Dublin Corporation) sit along Wood Quay where Viking long ships once moored a millennia ago.

FOLLOWING PAGE: An estimated 17,000 people protested Dublin Corporation's construction of its new offices on the site of a well-preserved Viking settlement at Wood Quay.

CITY COUNCIL
cathrach

Left: These buildings near Wood Quay are at the heart of what was Viking and medieval Dublin.

Right: The mosaic on the floor of City Hall incorporates the various symbols and emblems of Dublin.

OBEDIENTIA
FELICITAS
CIVIUM
URBIS

FAR LEFT: Christ Church was central to the old walled city. Although much altered in the nineteenth century, today it is one of the few surviving vestiges of medieval Dublin. *iStckphoto*

LEFT: Looking south on St. Nicholas Street; this would have been just outside the tenth century fortifications. Later stone walls were built further west, incorporating this area inside the protected city.

RIGHT: A thousand years ago, Dublin bay was host to Viking longships. These were tools of war and trade that allowed Norse communities to found cities and flourish on Ireland's shores for more than 200 years. This is the *Sea Stallion* of Glendalough starting out from Roskilde, Denmark for Dublin. *AFP/Getty Images*

FAR RIGHT: Dublin evolved as a significant Viking community. Longboats were constructed in Dublin for raids elsewhere. *Sea Stallion* is a replica of a Dublin-built ship on display at the Museum of Decorative Arts at Collins Barracks.

Left: A stone face adorns the outside of St. Patrick's Cathedral.

Right: Detail of the Steyne (Steine) Monument.

Left: Dublin Castle is an amalgamation of 800 years of architecture. Portions of the original Anglo-Norman structure have been blended with newer additions, renovations and rebuilding.

Right: St. Audoen's Church is one the oldest buildings in Dublin and its tower dates from the twelfth century. Located west of Christ Church, St. Audoen's sits near a vestige of the city walls near the old gate of the same name.

Georgian Dublin

Georgian Dublin

Over the centuries, campaigns by British adventurers, warlords, settlers and traders gradually tied the nations of Great Britain and Ireland together. In the sixteenth century, the Reformation in England under King Henry VIII resulted in the devastation of the Catholic powerbase in Ireland, conveyed significant church lands in and around Dublin to developers, and increased English power. In the mid-seventeenth century, violent civil war in Britain overflowed to Ireland. Cromwell's armies marauded through Ireland causing considerable devastation while further tightening British control.

Following Cromwell, Dublin flourished as the seat of government, trade, commerce and learning, as well as serving as a primary military staging point for Ireland. The fruits of Irish agriculture were directed through Dublin's ports to other parts of the growing British Empire. Ireland emerged as a key staging area for expansion of the Empire in the Americas. The wealth that flowed through Dublin in the late seventeenth and eighteenth centuries enabled visionary architects and planners to shape the city into one of the great urban conurbations of Europe. Dublin was home to the "Ascendancy"—Anglo-Irish gentry—the nation's ruling class, many of whom had resided in Ireland for generations. It also became home to an intellectual ascendancy, prosperous merchants and others who thrived in this bustling and rapidly growing city.

The nature of political control in Ireland imposed a socio-economic class-divide defined along religious and cultural lines. Whereas the ruling class enjoyed some of the finest urban living in Europe, many Gaelic-Irish lived in rural squalor. These differences resulted in tensions that boiled over from time to time. Yet, Irish politics were complex, and not rigidly formed along class lines: members of both rich and poor elements of Irish society were involved in various uprisings. For several hundred years, Ireland was torn by cycles of rebellion followed by harsh response from the authorities. Often conveyed largely as local events, in reality Irish Rebellions were tied to the international machinations of various Imperial powers. Ireland was a friction point between the strongest nations in Europe as they vied with one another for territorial, political and international supremacy.

As Dublin had evolved from Viking port to medieval garrison to Imperial seat of government, it gradually overflowed its walls like a boiling pot. Some changes were sudden, others imperceptible. Old buildings were replaced by new ones, while over the centuries street levels gradually rose by several feet, probably the result of an accumulation of debris dumped on the ground. Where medieval Dublin had grown in a haphazard fashion, from the late seventeenth century the city was carefully shaped by visionary planning. By design, Dublin expanded significantly east and north of the old town, the tidal estuary of the Liffey was systematically filled in, and building of quays on both north and south banks saw the Liffey straightened and channeled to its present course. Much of this quayside planning is credited to the Duke of Ormond, Lord Lieutenant of Dublin from 1666, who modeled his vision of Dublin on improvements in Paris.

In the Georgian period, Dublin underwent a multifaceted transformation as it entered a golden age of development. Significantly, the city was reshaped by visionary planners who implemented innovative street layouts, built whole new fashionable neighborhoods and set standards for elegant architectural styles that established a level of uniformity and grace on par with other great European cities.

Planning saw the creation of whole new residential neighborhoods, commercial development relocated and construction of key civic buildings east of the old city. Key to changes was the construction of new bridges and creation of significant new streets. There were substantial modifications to the old city as well, including the remodeling of Dublin Castle between 1685 and 1760 which saw portions of the old Norman structure demolished while others were absorbed into newer buildings. The construction of four bridges over the Liffey between 1670 and 1684 opened up the north side to rapid development from the late seventeenth century.

Dublin's population soared during the Georgian period. In 1700 it had but 60,000 inhabitants. By 1800 this had climbed to roughly 182,000 and, in 1841—on the eve of the catastrophe known as the Great Famine—Dublin counted nearly 232,800 people within its boundaries. As in the twenty-first century, eighteenth century Dublin suffered from acute congestion in the city center as result of rapid growth and the inadequacies of old streets to new patterns of commerce. The narrowness of the old streets was ill-suited to the growing numbers of horse-drawn carriages. Street traders, markets and fairs made the old city a navigational quagmire. Key to

Previous page: The iconic Liffey Bridge—Ha'Penny Bridge—is a design credited to John Windsor. Cast in Dublin and erected in 1816, the bridge was completely overhauled and rededicated in December 2001.

Right: In its day, Dublin's Henrietta Street was one of the city's most exclusive addresses. By the mid-nineteenth century, its once luxurious terraced houses had been subdivided as multi-family tenement apartments.

Georgian planning was the establishment of the Wide Streets Commission in 1757—that, for the next century, set guidelines for the development of broad streets, elegant architectural styles and well-placed buildings with uniform frontage following a classical design. This was in contrast to the narrow winding alleys, awkwardly placed buildings and unenlightened architecture of the medieval city.

Among the seventeenth century Liffey spans was the stone arched Essex Bridge (today Grattan Bridge) that connected Capel Street with the old city. Although a significant improvement, congestion was especially bad on the south side of the new bridge as the twisting narrow streets that reached it were incapable of accommodating the increased flow of traffic. In light of this, in 1762, the Irish Parliament allocated funds for construction of a new direct thoroughfare reaching directly from Essex Bridge toward the gates of Dublin Castle. This was Parliament Street, named to honor the body that authorized and financed its construction, and it replaced the old streets of Cork Hill and Blind Alley which required the clearing away of many old buildings that, as might be expected, caused some controversy. At the top of Parliament Street, the Royal Exchange was built in front of the Castle—and not far from the former black pool that had given Dublin its name. Architect Thomas Cooley was awarded the job of designing the new building. Today, it serves as Dublin City Hall. The vista looking down Capel Street, across the Grattan Bridge and down Parliament Street to Cooley's masterpiece, exemplifies the vision of the Wide Street Commission's first success. It continued with its improvements. Among them was the broadening and redevelopment of Dame Street and College Green, east of Dublin Castle.

Among the significant projects implemented by the Wide Streets Commission was the construction of Carlisle Bridge over the Liffey in 1794, along with broad

LEFT: The faded glory of seventeenth century terraced houses and cobblestone pavement on Henrietta Street on Dublin's north side is one of the city's great contrasts.

new streets that connected it on both sides of the river. The construction of Liffey bridges had the effect of pushing Dublin's port eastward by limiting the ability of sailing ships to navigate the river. Building Carlisle Bridge moved the closest mooring points half a mile downriver. This roughly coincided with the construction of a magnificent new Custom House between 1781 and 1791—situated on the north bank of the Liffey in an area previously occupied by little more than mucky tidal flats. Since 1707, the Custom House had been located upriver on the south bank near present day Wellington Quay.

The changes were necessary to accommodate the growing volume of shipping but proved unpopular with prominent Dublin firms negatively affected by the move. Although convenient to businesses in the old city, this older Custom House had become a limitation to trade because of inadequate space on the quays. (Many businessmen, however, may have argued that the Custom House was limiting trade because of the duties it assessed to goods passing through Dublin port!) Equally significant, and also unpopular, was the role Carlisle Bridge played in establishing a new north-south thoroughfare. Designed to connect the area defined by Dublin's Parliament building (constructed opposite Trinity College between 1729 and 1739, now owned by the Bank of Ireland) with Luke Gardiner's recent residential developments, the new streets emerged as Dublin's primary commercial district that effectively shifted the both axis and location of city center east from the old city. The original Carlisle Bridge was just a third the width of the present structure which was significantly rebuilt and enlarged in the 1880s. It was renamed O'Connell Bridge in the 1920s and remains at the heart of the city center.

A principle architect for Dublin's late eighteenth century development was James Gandon, a transplanted Englishman. Gandon's mastery of classic design was well suited to the vision of Dublin's Georgian planners. Among his works were Carlisle Bridge, the Custom House, the Irish Law Courts (now the Four Courts) and Kings Inns. He also participated in a re-design and expansion of Ireland's Parliament building.

Significant upscale residential development on the north side began early in the eighteenth century, several decades prior to the Wide Streets Commission. Especially significant were new neighborhoods laid out on estates owned by the senior Luke Gardiner. His development on Henrietta Street, dating to about 1730, saw architect Sir Edward Lovett Pearce design fine stately terraced homes for some of Dublin's wealthiest families. In its day, Gardiner's Henrietta Street was one of the best places to live in Ireland. This prototype Georgian Street set the tone for future residential development on both north and south sides of Dublin later in the century. Gardiner also developed the Sackville Mall. This was later extended as Sackville Street, which became Dublin's widest thoroughfare, and is today known as O'Connell Street.

Key to Dublin's high-end residential development are its five great squares which emerged as some of the city's fanciest neighborhoods. First was the development of St. Stephen's Green in the second half of the seventeenth century by the Dublin Corporation—the municipal body with royal authority that had traditionally been responsible for the maintenance and planning of city infrastructure. The largest of Dublin's five great squares, St. Stephen's Green was the prototype for the later squares, and its planning predates the Wide Streets Commission—as well as the other squares—by nearly a century. Whereas St. Stephen's Green was built around what had been a public common, the four classic Georgian squares were carved out of private estates and were largely private development schemes. On the north side, Rutland Square (today Parnell Square) was designed in 1755, while Gardiner Square—later Mountjoy Square—was built between 1792 and 1818. (Both names

BELOW: After the Act of Union in 1800, the Bank of Ireland bought this neo-classical building originally constructed for Ireland's Parliament. It is still owned by the bank and today's Irish Parliament—"Dáil Éireann"—meets at Leinster House on Kildare Street.

honor the Gardiners who inherited the Mountjoy title in the eighteenth century.) On the south side, Merrion Square was laid out by architect John Ensor beginning in 1762. It is named for the sixth Lord Fitzwilliam of Meryon, and considered the most perfectly executed of the five squares. The terraced houses along its northern side were built first and these elegant old homes retain an air of majesty to this day. Last, and smallest of the great squares is Fitzwilliam Square, begun in 1791 and completed 36 years later.

Noted for their classic aesthetic, Dublin's great squares are famous for their residents as well as their architecture. Among Mountjoy Square's most famous residents were playwright Seán O'Casey and literary giant James Joyce whose early twentieth century works are part of the fabric of Dublin lore. While Merrion Square was residence for many Irish parliamentarians in heyday, some of Dublin's best known citizens have also had homes here over the years. Among them were politician Daniel O'Connell; Ireland's most famous poet William Butler Yeats; and flamboyant Victorian playwright Oscar Wilde.

The Georgian squares were only part of the greater development of landlords' estates. Of these, the properties of Gardiner and Fitzwilliam families were the most significant which remains evident today as not only the squares, but key Georgian streets still carry names honoring their proprietors.

Part of the vision of Dublin's planners was the distinction of buildings through architectural style. Where civil structures embodied neo-classic design, residential buildings are marked by subdued elegance. Key to Georgian Dublin are its classic brick terraced houses. With many variations on the theme, these are

characterized by three or four storey red brick construction. The front of the building features rows of windows of equal width above one another, but progressively shorter to give the whole of the building an illusion of greater height. Distinctive to Dublin's houses are the front entrance: the door painted a uniform primary color is flanked by faux-classical colonnades with side windows, and topped with a semi-circular fan-shaped window. The repetition of the essential terrace design allowed for nominal and subtle variations in detail, so each house is unique, yet consistent in style with those around it. Impressive rows of Georgian houses, standing like soldiers to attention, lined the great eighteenth and early nineteenth century streets and squares. Most notable is Fitzwilliam Street that connects Merrion Square, Fitzwilliam Square and Lesson Street. Although only a little more than a half mile in length, this inspiring tangent with parallel flanks of uninterrupted terraced houses was known as the "Georgian Mile". Despite public vandalism in the early 1960s, when Ireland's Electrical Supply Board carved out more than two dozen houses to build their modern office block, the effect can still be appreciated today.

Improvements to both ground and water transport were key features of Dublin's eighteenth century development. Not only were Dublin's streets straightened and enlarged, but roads in the countryside were improved as well. A map of Ireland from the period clearly reveals most major roads radiated from Dublin. The Turnpike Act of 1727 specified minimum width requirements for Irish toll roads. Ultimately some 1,500 miles of toll highway were built on the island. Ireland entered the canal era in 1756 when construction of the Grand Canal began along a course south of the city center. The first portion of this canal opened to traffic in 1779 and, by 1805, it effectively provided a trans-Irish conduit connecting Dublin with the Shannon. The Royal Canal was the second significant canal system. It began construction in 1789 with the first segments opened to traffic nine years later. This ran north of the city center, roughly mirroring the path of the Grand Canal in Dublin.

Key trends to Dublin's development over the last thousand years has been the gradual relocation of the port ever further east, combined with the filling of land along the banks of the Liffey, followed by redevelopment of old port areas for other uses. In Viking times, Dublin's port was at the very center of commerce, located at the heart of the settlement, the Dubh Linn, from which the city is named. In Norman times, the use of larger ships moved the port to the Liffey estuary. As the size of ships continued to grow and volume of commerce became more intensive, it was necessary to move the port closer to Dublin Bay. Thus the need to relocate the Custom House as described earlier.

While Dublin harbor was key to the city's prosperity, for centuries shipping had been plagued by heavy winds, strong currents and a dangerous shifting sand bar in Dublin Bay, as well as large sand bars north and south of Liffey mouth known as "bulls".

Between 1714 and 1728, construction of the North Wall and East Wall between the north bank of the Liffey and the River Tolka were significant steps undertaken to improve the harbor that included massive land reclamation and the construction of new quays. However, the most significant improvement was construction the Great South Wall, to shelter ships transiting Dublin Bay. This massive engineering project was undertaken mid-century, and extended a sea wall more than two and a half miles into the Bay. Development of significant suburban deepwater harbors in the early nineteenth century were aimed at providing safe harbors for passenger and mail ships which had continued to experience difficulties navigating the windy shallow waters of Dublin Bay. North of Dublin, at Howth, a new harbor was built in 1818 while, about the same time, celebrated British engineer John Rennie constructed a deepwater harbor at Dún Laoghaire (sometimes spelled Dunleary to reflect its anglicized pronunciation). This would serve passenger ships and the fast mail ships known as "Packets" (in *A History of the Port of Dublin*, W.A. Gilligan attributes this eighteenth century term as being derived from "Pacquets of Letters"). Following a royal visit at the opening of the port, Dún Laoghaire was renamed Kingstown from 1821 although it reverted in the 1920s. Kingstown grew in importance following the opening of Ireland's first railway, the Dublin and Kingstown Railway (D&KR) in 1834. Continued expansion and improvements to Dublin port have continued through to the present day.

In 1759, Arthur Guinness purchased the Rainsford Brewery where he began brewing "porter", a popular variety of dark ale now known as stout for which the Guinness name has become famous. The rich tasting beer has long been popular with Dublin residents. Among the distinctive characteristics of Guinness stout appeared to be its unusual sensitivity to travel as well as the way it's stored and poured. For this reason, connoisseurs of stout engage in frequent discussion about which Dublin pubs deliver the best product. Guinness emerged as not only the most successful brewer in Dublin but throughout Ireland. Key to the success of Guinness was the perfection of a superior product combined with eighteenth century transport improvements. Access to the Grand Canal allowed the stout to reach a national market as, for nearly 200 years, Guinness traveled to pubs by canal boat. In more recent years, Guinness was among the largest rail freight shippers in Ireland, however, despite the proximity of sidings to the brewery, Guinness shipped its last kegs by rail in 2006. Now Guinness bounces along on the nation's congested highways. Historically, the Guinness family has been generous with gifts to the city including opening St. Stephen's Green to the public in the 1870s (it had long been a park for the exclusive use of nearby residents), the creation of the Iveagh Gardens off Harcourt Street, and the restoration of St. Patrick's Cathedral and construction of adjacent parks.

LEFT: Among Dublin's most recognizable buildings is the main entrance of Trinity College on College Green, built during the 1750s.

Right: The heart of Georgian Dublin was College Green where the Trinity College (right) faced the neo-classical Irish Parliament (left). Asphalt now covers the old green.

LEFT: Among the noteworthy features of Trinity College's Parliament Square is the bell tower known as the Campanile, a unique structure dating to the 1850s.

RIGHT: The north side of Merrion Square is one of the foremost examples of Georgian terraced house architecture.

ATLAS

TWI
International
TEXTILE
MANUFACTURING
SUPPLIERS
25
EDWARD DILLON & CO. LIMITED

LEFT: Mountjoy Square, originally known as Gardiner Square, suffered precipitous decline after the Act of Union. After nearly two centuries of decay, the square is finally getting the attention it deserves.

RIGHT: This impressive church looms over passers by on the northwest corner of Parnell Square.

LEFT: Hues of sunset tinge the southern sky above chimneys on Merrion Street Upper.

RIGHT: The proximity to the Dáil places the corner of Merrion Street Upper and Merrion Row near the heart of the Republic's government. Nearby pubs and cafes are frequented by the movers and shakers of the Irish nation.

REILLYS BAR
GUINNESS
GUINNESS
Bagel FACTORY
Bagel FACTORY

Left: Mountjoy Square was one of two Georgian Squares on Dublin's north side. Once famous for its tenements, the square survived decades of neglect.

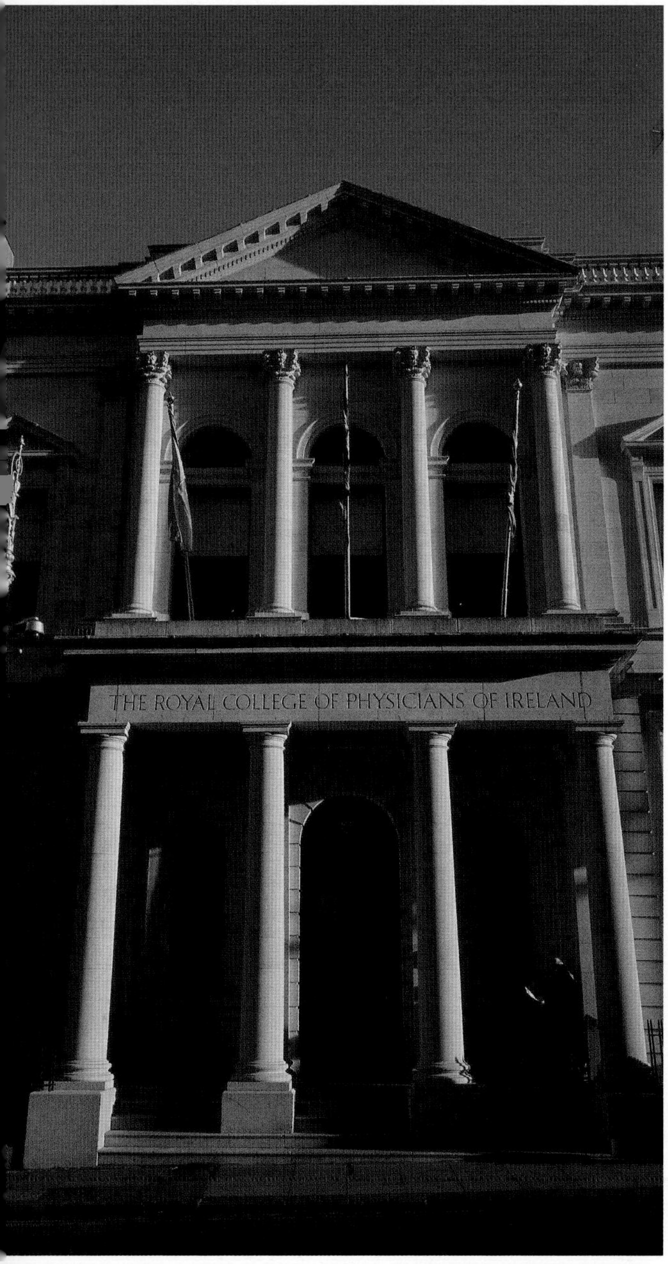

LEFT: Just a few doors down from the National Library on Kildare Street is the Royal College of Physicians of Ireland, housed in this fine neo-classic building designed by W.G. Murray.

RIGHT: Dublin is often described as the foremost Georgian city. Ironically, it was decades of impoverishment that put the city in an architectural time warp. The "Celtic Tiger" has finally allowed the restoration of many fine eighteenth century terrace houses.

FAR RIGHT: Simplicity, symmetry and repetition with subtle variations give the Georgian terraced houses an intrinsic elegance. Mountjoy Square has some of the finest examples of this style in Dublin.

LEFT: The smallest, last and best preserved of Dublin's five Georgian squares is Fitzwilliam Square on the city's south side.

RIGHT: Georgian terraced houses on Leeson Street.

66

FAR LEFT: A trademark of Dublin's Georgian terraced houses is the fan shaped window, or fanlight, above the front door.

LEFT: The Kings Inns, located at the end of Henrietta Street, was James Gandon's final neo-classical work in Dublin and not finished until 1817.

RIGHT: The copper capped Four Courts is among Dublin's icons. Built from 1786 to 1802, the building was damaged in the Irish Civil War and restored by the Irish Free State.

LEFT: Begun in the late seventeenth century, the old Royal Hospital at Kilmainham was the design of Sir William Robinson. It is now paradoxically home to the Irish Museum of Modern Art.

RIGHT: Spanning 138 feet, Dublin's Liffey Bridge—popularly known as the Ha'Penny Bridge—is the oldest cast iron arch bridge in Ireland. It is seen in spring 1999, before its extensive overhaul as part of a millennium-related city center tidy-up.

TO LET
2 SHOPS
IGNS NOW

LEFT: Linking popular north side shopping areas with Temple Bar, the Ha'Penny Bridge is clogged with pedestrians at peak periods. During the Christmas shopping frenzy it can take up to five minutes to negotiate the crowded span.

BELOW: The geometry of the terraced house is typified here on Leeson Street. Georgian planning allowed for widespread creation of uniform architectural designs that gave eighteenth century Dublin its character.

RIGHT: Leeson Street Lower sign in Irish and English, above the old cast iron Mansion House Ward plate marker on the side of an eighteenth century residence.

SEEING TOURS
OPSTYLE FURNITURE

Left: Dublin's Mellowes Bridge—built in 1768—completes a north-south thoroughfare of Queen Street on the north side and Bridgefoot Street on the south side. Originally called the Queen's Bridge, it was renamed in 1942.

LEFT: In the eighteenth century, transport from Dublin to the Midlands was improved by the construction of two canal systems. Water reflects a dull sky at the No. 6 locks on the Royal Canal at Glasnevin.

RIGHT: Guinness's St. James Street Brewery often fills surrounding neighborhoods with the aroma of roasting barley. How much longer international drinks company Diagio will retain this historic facility has been a subject of speculation.

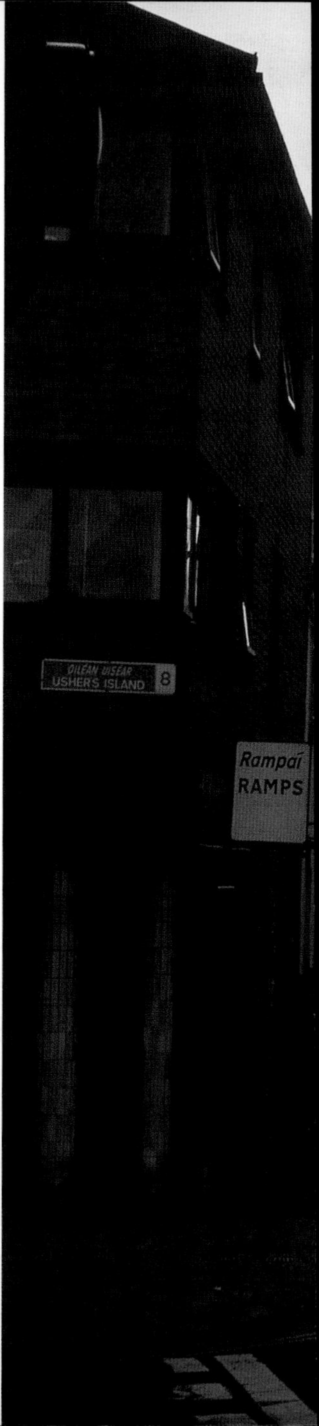

GUINNESS
WHISKEY
Off-Licence
Off-Licence

1759
GUINNESS

LEFT: In 1759, Arthur Guinness established one of Dublin's most famous addresses. Today, St. James's Gate is synonymous with dark, creamy stout, best enjoyed at any of Dublin's many fine public houses.

RIGHT: Often heralded as Dublin's finest structure, James Gandon's Custom House is a well balanced adaptation of neo-classic design on the north quays east of the city center.

FOLLOWING PAGE: The Irish High Court—known as the Four Courts—was designed by James Gandon, who blended the work of Thomas Cooley with his own neo-classical style.

Left: Parnell Square—originally Rutland Square—is immediately north of O'Connell Street. Here majestic terraced houses display their Georgian architectural styles so closely associated with Dublin.

Right: Detail of the Custom House dome: atop is a statue representing Commerce.

LEFT: Situated adjacent to Dublin Castle on Dame Street, the old Royal Exchange has served as City Hall since 1852. Twelve Corinthian columns support the dome over the rotunda.

RIGHT: A view looking up at the dome at Dublin City Hall. Thomas Cooley's well executed design was completed in 1779 for use as the Royal Exchange.

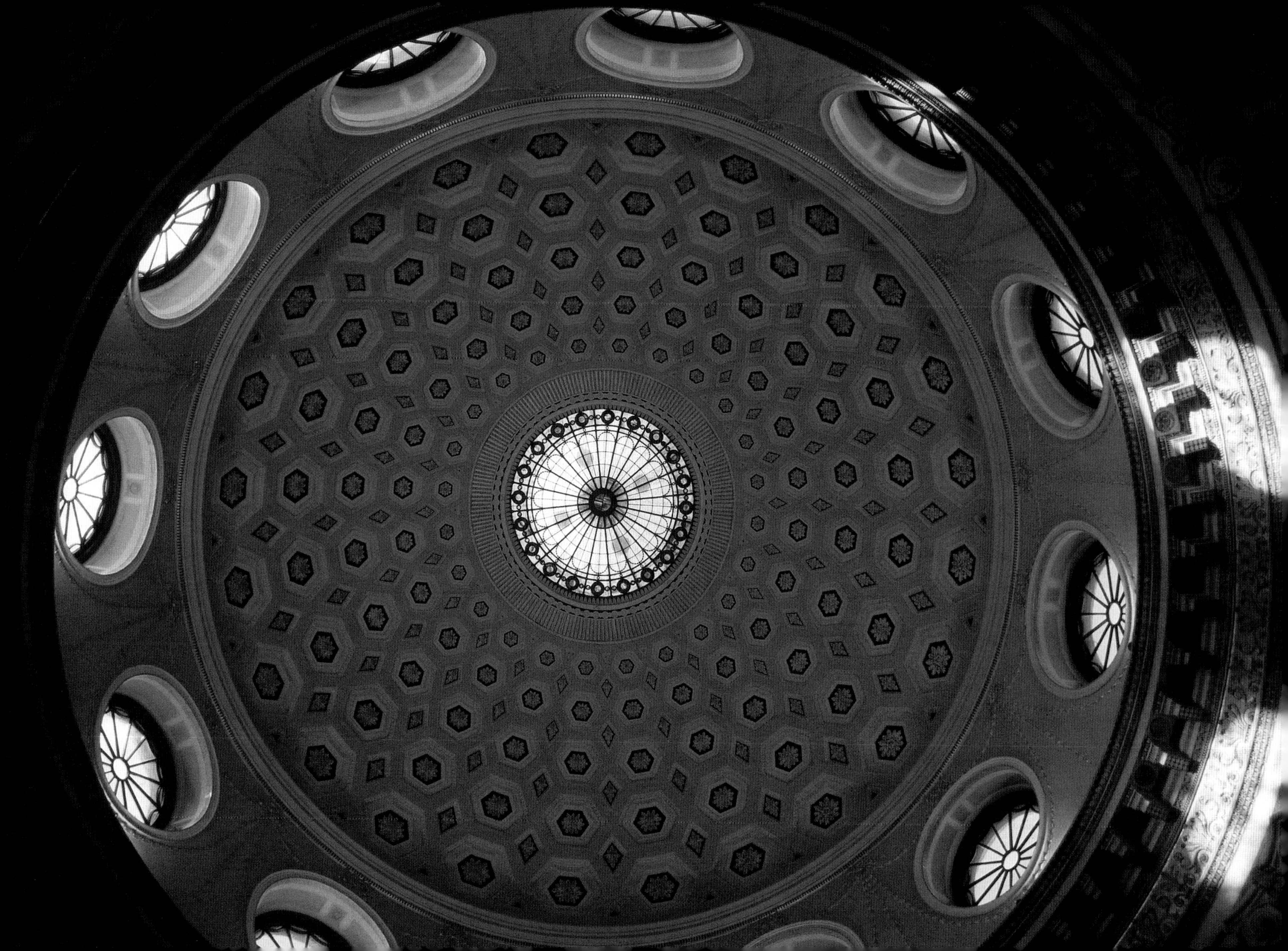

LEFT: The old Royal Barracks, later renamed Collins Barracks, were designed by Thomas Burgh. Opened in the early eighteenth century, these were once deemed the largest enclosed drilling ground in Europe; now it houses the Museum of Decorative Arts.

RIGHT: Merrion Street Upper, once the residence of the Duke of Wellington, is now largely made up of offices, including those of the Irish government's Department of Finance on the left.

HOWTH

LEFT: The Guinness brewery complex along St. James Street has been in the family's hands since December 1759 when Arthur Guinness signed a 9,000-year lease at an annual rent of £45. Here, men loading barges in 1940. *Time & Life Pictures/ Getty Images*

ABOVE: Cast iron sign for the old Trinity Ward on Merrion Street.

RIGHT: Considered by many the masterwork of English architect James Gandon, the Custom House is well executed in the neo-classical style that typified public buildings of the Georgian period.

Left: Trinity College's impressive Palladian façade is credited to architect Theodore Jacobsen. On the left is the old Irish Parliament building, made redundant with the Act of Union and now the Bank of Ireland.

Right: The National Museum on Kildare Street is adjacent to Leinster House. Inside, numerous national treasures and historic artifacts are displayed.

MUSEUM

Victorian and Edwardian Dublin

Victorian and Edwardian Dublin

In the nineteenth century, the character and demographics of the city changed radically. History defined Dublin's changes as events and trends shaped the city.

The American Revolution in the late 1770s inspired similar aspirations in both France and Ireland. Following the French Revolution of 1789, growing unrest culminated in the Irish rebellion of 1798. Led by both Catholic and Protestants at various levels of society, the rebellion was notably aided by French forces—much to the horror of British authorities, who not only feared war with France but were dismayed with that country's recent anti-royal blood-letting and were distrustful of mutual sympathy between these two nations of disenfranchised Catholics. British reaction was swift, and Irish rebellion was crushed by the British military. However, concerns of further Irish discord led to the Act of Union in 1800. This fundamental change removed the government of Ireland from Dublin and, for more than a century, Ireland was ruled from London. The Act of Union ended Dublin's golden Georgian age and a period of decline set in.

Many of the richest families either followed the trail of power to London or, tired of urban living, left Dublin for their palatial country estates. Yet there were other changes, too. Conclusion of the Napoleonic Wars by the second decade calmed fears, enabling the political successes of Daniel O'Connell who improved conditions for Ireland's Catholic majority from the 1820s onward. New opportunities bolstered the rise of a new Catholic middle class.

The growing industrialization of Britain had its effects on Ireland. Where Britain was blessed with significant deposits of coal and iron, Ireland was not. And Britain's broad-based industrial economy was in contrast with Ireland's traditional agricultural base that put its people at an economic disadvantage. As a result, Dublin stagnated in the nineteenth century. Equally important to the city were related shifts—suburban development followed by a rising tide of the desperately poor, hungry and largely unskilled rural masses pouring into the city during the Great Famine of the 1840s.

Ireland's first railway, the Dublin and Kingstown Railway (D&KR) opened in 1834 and this coastal line is often cited as the world's first suburban railway; in other words, a line used by daily commuters. Whereas Britain's early railways were largely freight haulers to facilitate industrial development, from its beginning the D&KR allowed affluent Dubliners to commute by train from seaside homes over what was then a considerable distance to their places of employment in the city center. This was one step in a trend of affluent suburbanization of Dublin. The success of the D&KR, as well as railways in Britain, inspired a railway-building boom in Ireland. A myriad of railway lines reached out to towns and villages throughout the island. Like the road network, these were largely Dublin oriented. However, most of these later lines were not intended as suburban railways but built as intercity routes. A variety of terminals served Dublin, among them D&KR's Westland Row (Pearse Station since 1966), located east of Trinity College. On the north side, terminals were built at the North Wall, Amiens Street (Connolly Station since 1966), and at Broadstone near the Kings Inn. On the south side, Kingsbridge Station (Heuston Station since 1966) served as the terminal for the Great Southern & Western Railway. Another small railway terminal was constructed at Harcourt Street, not far from the St. Stephen's Green, which served the Harcourt Street line of the Dublin and South Eastern. Although Dublin's railways suffered from retrenchment in the twentieth century, its three remaining active main stations (Pearse, Connolly and Heuston) qualify as the oldest continuously operated city railway terminals in the world.

Prior to the Famine, Dublin had reached a population of more than 232,700 people, while boundaries of the city pushed outward toward the canals. By mid-century, affluent Dubliners were seeking suburban addresses in ever greater numbers in townships along the D&KR such as Sandymount, Black Rock and Kingstown. In addition, a number of new townships were formed on the periphery of the city. Ballsbridge, Rathmines, Ranelagh and Harold's Cross developed beyond the Grand Canal. To the west, Kilmainham—long home to the Royal Hospital—swelled with suburban development, as did north side neighborhoods at Drumcondra, Cabra and Clontarf. Change didn't occur overnight, but over the course of generations. By the end of the nineteenth century, Dublin city center was notorious for its slums.

The decay was shocking, and especially poignant because so many poor Irish were living in squalor in neighborhoods that had once thrived as the nicest in Europe. Once-desirable mansions on Henrietta Street and Mountjoy Square had been sold and subdivided into squalid tenement apartments where large families lived packed in together. Disease was rampant. Typhoid, cholera and tuberculosis claimed thousands of lives. In 1900,

Previous page: Dublin's most famous hotel is the Shelbourne which faces St. Stephen's Green at its northeast corner.

Right: Built along South Great George's Street, Dublin's South City Markets were originally constructed in the 1870s and rebuilt in 1892 following a disastrous fire.

THE GRAFTON House
FUTONS
ORIENTAL EMPORIUM
FUTON STORE
LASER
NEW BODYFORM WITH EFFICAPT
ROAD

Dublin had the highest death rate of any city in western Europe, nearly twice that of London.

To many, the seething Dublin slums seemed emblematic of the inequities of Imperialism, and represented everything that was wrong with British rule in Ireland. Although Dublin's problems were acute, the city was not unique; its pattern of decay would be repeated many times over in other cities in other countries. Dublin suffered from a vicious circle. Politics aside, as Dublin's most affluent residents moved away, and its middle classes fled to the suburbs, the inner city became filled by those with the least resources, and in much greater numbers than before. The Dublin Corporation which managed municipal affairs was faced with the dual problem of declining resources and ever greater demands. Also, as conditions in the inner city got worse, the impetus for those with means to move away from the center was greater. Complicating matters for Dubliners were real and perceived cultural, religious and financial divisions that allowed people of different classes and neighborhoods to distinguish between themselves and added to the gulf between the poor and those with means.

Culture and commerce never deserted Dublin, however. The nineteenth century was not all gloom and squalor: many of Dublin's finer buildings were erected during this period and there were thriving healthy areas despite the slums. Many fine Victorian buildings remain in the city center and across Dublin. In 1879, the Star of Erin Music Hall opened on Dame Street, near the location of the original black pool. This classic Victorian stage retains its multiple balconies, and is today known as the Olympia Theater. Its original iron entrance canopy survived until a few years ago when it was struck by an errant motorist. It has since been restored. Not far away on Parliament Street and across from the Grattan Bridge is the Sunlight Chambers—an exquisitely detailed Victorian structure. Built around 1900, the second floor displays a series of colorful pictorial friezes that relay the history of hygiene in tableau. The Grattan Bridge is essentially another Victorian creation. Although the basic structure dates to about 1676, and was substantially rebuilt in 1753, it was rebuilt again in 1875 when cast and wrought iron footpaths—adorned with decorative iron hippocampus statuettes—were added to widen the arch supported roadway.

During this period, Grafton Street and its environs flourished with a variety of commercial interests—some still thriving there today. Among long-standing Grafton Street businesses is the department store started in 1848 by proprietors John Brown and James Thomas. The present store is actually across the street from the original premises, but today Brown Thomas is one of Dublin's most famous businesses. Other Victorian shopping districts include the South City Markets and its famous covered Market Arcade with its turreted red brick façade facing South Great George's Street. Camden and Thomas Streets also flourished.

Dublin has long been famous for its distinctive and convivial public houses, intrinsic to its social fabric and lively nightlife. The format of Dublin's traditional pubs today has a Victorian flavor. A number of significant pubs survive from Victorian times, albeit with varying degrees of remodeling and improvement. Some favorites are located on streets and alleys off Grafton Street or nearby: Neary's—officially the Chatham Lounge—known for its classic bicameral arrangement and snugs; the Stag's Head on Dame Court is a multilevel affair that dates to 1894; and McDaid's on Harry Street dates from the Georgian period and is famous for its twentieth century literary patrons, among them Brendan Behan. An enthusiastic patron staggering out of McDaid's will be sure to note the premises across the street operated as Bruxelles which has a classic 1890s façade designed by Dublin's most prolific pub architects, J.J. O'Callaghan. Elsewhere in Dublin,

LEFT AND FAR LEFT: Ireland's National Library is situated in Kildare Street, Dublin. The interior image shows dome of the reading room. *Both: IIC/ Axiom/Getty Images*

Mulligan's on Poolbeg Street retains classic Victorian splendor, as does the Long Hall on South Great George's Street. A gem of an old north side pub is Kavanagh's, adjacent to Gate 6 at the Glasnevin Cemetery, better known as the 'Gravediggers', which has been featured on film and television over the years. However, many pubs that embody Victorian style are recreations, while other old pubs bear little resemblance to their actual nineteenth century décor. Yet, it is the vibe of the patrons and staff more than wooden paneling, soft lighting and a well polished bar that give a pub its flavor.

RIGHT: South of Dublin, "Dún Laoghaire" was developed after the Napoleonic Wars as a port for passenger and mail ships. Today it is a primary ferry port connecting Dublin and Holyhead.

FAR RIGHT: Cast iron hippocampi adorn the Grattan Bridge—built on the location of the seventeenth century Essex Bridge.

LEFT, RIGHT AND FOLLOWING PAGE: On the corner of Parliament Street and Essex Quay are the Sunlight Chambers. Built about 1900, this ornate building features detailed tableau relief that portrays a history of hygiene.

RIGHT: Located south of the Grand Canal, the Rathmines township grew rapidly in Victorian times. It was finally annexed by Dublin in the 1930s. The enormous church dome seen here can be spotted from the air when landing at Dublin airport.

Far left: Shelbourne Hotel's eclectic architecture is in contrast with the stately reserve of the Georgian terraced houses in the area.

Left: This bronze angel by John Henry Foley on the O'Connell Monument represents the classical figure of Eloquence.

Right: 1933 aerial view of Dublin. In the center of the picture is the Parliament building; above and left the National Library. *Hulton/Getty Images*

RIGHT: Closed to traffic in 1959, Dublin's Harcourt Street railroad station has housed a popular bar and entertainment venues in recent years.

FAR RIGHT: In 2004, a portion of the Harcourt Street railroad line was reopened as the LUAS Green line. Trams now stop in front of the old station; in the old days trains served platforms inside the station.

LEFT: Ornamental cast iron detail of the old Harcourt Street railroad station.

RIGHT: Kingsbridge Station served as the main passenger terminal and offices for the Great Southern and Western Railway.

VIII VIC

Left: Designed in 1845 by Sancton Wood, Kingsbridge Station was renamed in 1966 for Seán Heuston, martyred for his role in the 1916 Easter Rising.

Right: The Victorian brick buildings of the Iveagh Trust are opposite St. Patrick's Park, both sponsored by Lord Iveagh of the Guinness brewing family.

Following page: Last used for freight around 1960, the Grand Canal in Dublin occasionally hosts pleasure craft, although it's rare to see boats navigating the locks.

RIASC
RIASC

LEFT: Claude Road on Dublin's north side is a quiet residential neighborhood that largely escaped the decay of decades past.

RIGHT: Call in for a drink after work; John Mulligan's pub on Poolbeg Street is among the city's most famous and exudes a classic charm associated with Victorian Dublin.

WINES
EST. 1782
WHISKEY

RIGHT: The Portabello owes its name to its location along the Grand Canal. It's a popular haunt for supporters of the Gaelic Athletic Association.

PORTOBELLO
33

Left: Some of the most perfect pints can be found in the virtual shadow of the Guinness Brewery. Fallon's pub on Dean Street is a charming local pub known for good stout.

Right: James Joyce posed a puzzle: how to walk through Dublin without passing a pub. The trick is revealed here inside Reilly's Bar on Merrion Street Upper.

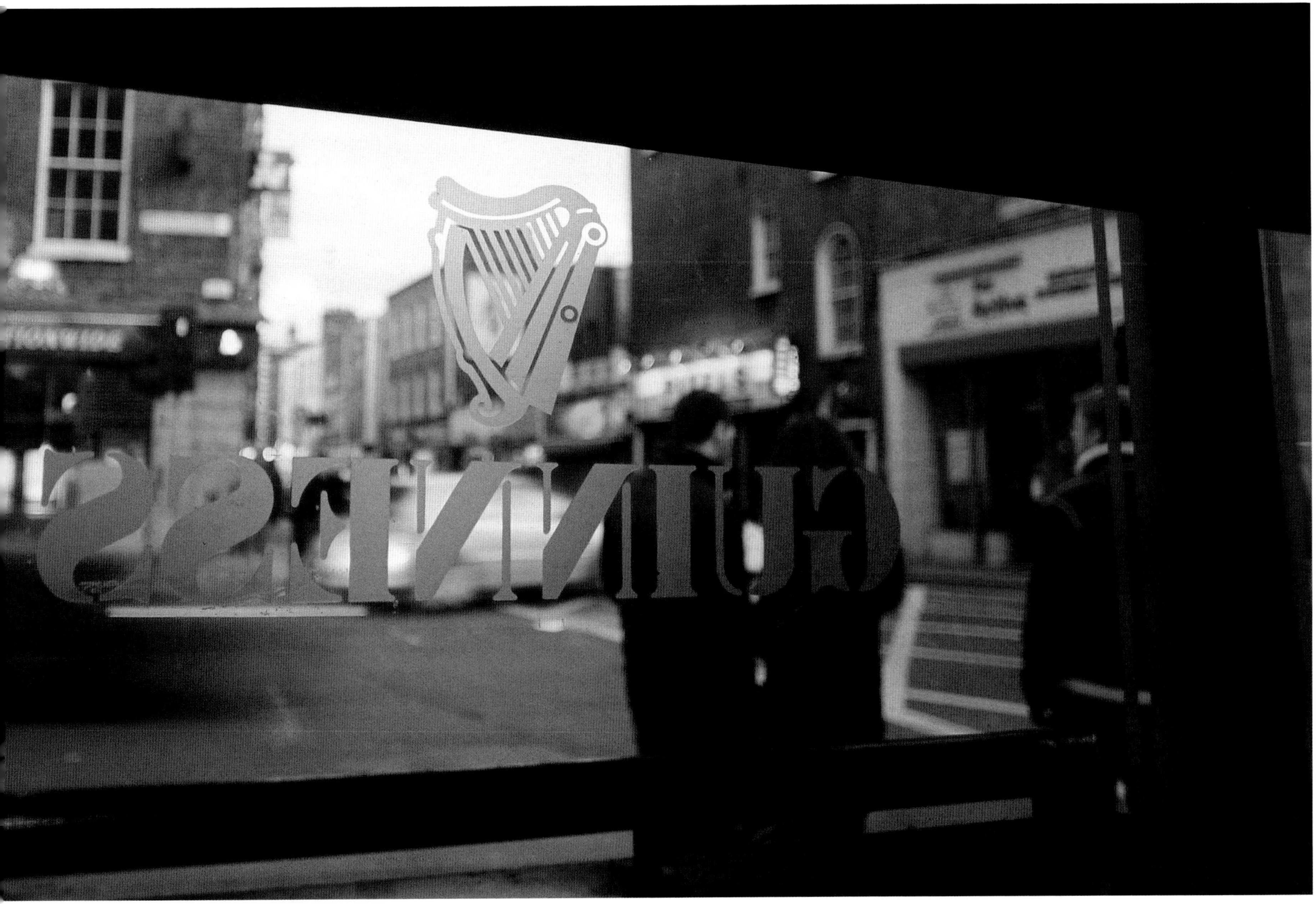
GUINNESS

Left: Silhouettes of cast iron hippocampi on the footpath railing of the Grattan Bridge. Evening sun graces buildings along Ormond Quay in the distance.

Right: Like ghosts of Dublin's past, haunted bronze forms walk wearily toward coffin ships on the Dublin Quays. In the 1840s, the Great Famine saw tens of thousands of starving men, women and children descend upon Dublin.

LEFT: Among Dublin's defining contrasts are present day prosperity and the tragedy of the Famine as emphasized by this modern statue.

RIGHT: Among Dublin's best known public houses, Doheny & Nesbitt on Baggot Street Lower has had a number of famous guests over the years, among them former Soviet Premier Mikhail Gorbachev.

FOLLOWING PAGE: Opened in 1834, the station at Westland Row—Pearse Station since 1966—is credited for being the world's oldest continuously-served big-city railroad station. The shed dates to 1884, while completion of the Loop Line in 1891 made it a through station.

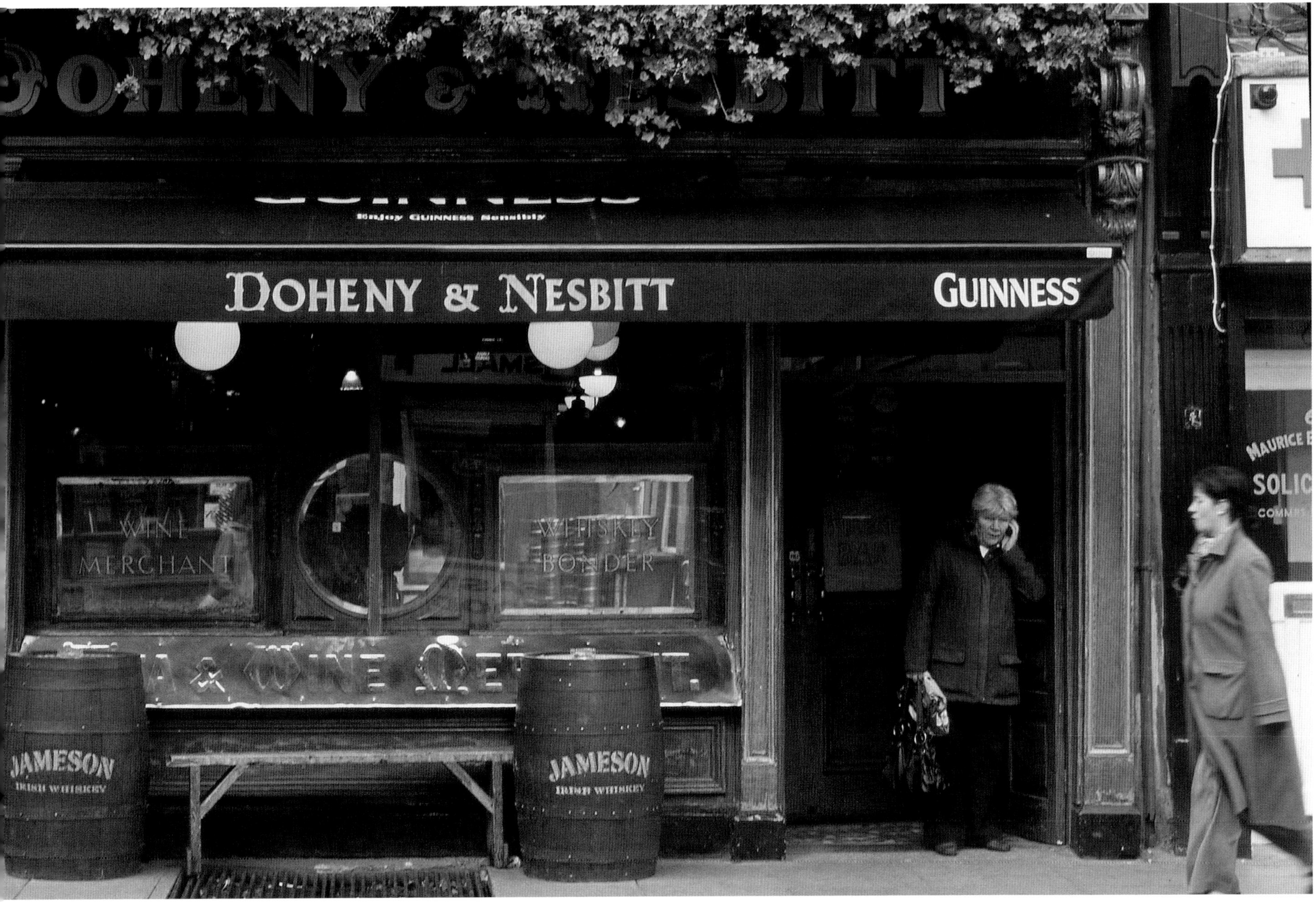
DOHENY & NESBITT
GUINNESS
WINE MERCHANT
WHISKEY BONDER
JAMESON
IRISH WHISKEY
JAMESON
IRISH WHISKEY

SAVE WIT
Stn. na bPiarsach
PEARSE
8312
DART
DUBLIN AREA RAPID TRANSIT

LENT IS WHAT YOU DO
TRÓCAIRE
Giving i aring in Action
EXIT

Left: Despite economic declines in the nineteenth century, Dublin's city center continued to thrive commercially. It remains vital today and this jewelry shop on Johnson Court Alley off Grafton Street is among dozens of businesses in the area.

Right: Doheny & Nesbitt is among Dublin's finest Victorian pubs.

Far right: Toners on Baggot Street Lower is another classic Dublin pub, famous as the only pub that poet W.B. Yeats ever visited, and briefly at that.

DOHENY
MANGAN
GROUP
NESBITT

TONERS
A PUB
GUINNESS
HARP

LEFT: John Kavanagh's classic old bar and rustic atmosphere has changed little with the years. A visit to the "The Gravediggers" is a refreshing step back in time from the maelstrom of modern Dublin.

RIGHT: Established in 1833, John Kavanagh's pub known as "The Gravediggers" has been the site of films and television over the years.

LEFT: McDade's is a fine old pub, legendary as the haunt of Dublin wordsmith Brendan Behan. Reflected in McDaid's windows is Bruxelles, located across Harry Street.

RIGHT: At St. Stephen's Green southeast corner, this bronze depicts the three Fates. The bronze was a gift to Ireland from the Federal Republic of Germany as thanks for Ireland's aid to German children following the Second World War.

FAR RIGHT: In the 1916 Rising, Countess Markiewicz led her troops into St. Stephen's Green. She is remembered at the Green by this bronze bust by artist Seamus Murphy.

CONSTANCE
MARKIEVICZ
MAJOR
IRISH CITIZEN ARMY
1916

LEFT: Among St. Stephen's Green attractions are its gorgeous flowerbeds.

Dublin from Irish Independence

1831
1915
Ó DONNABÁIN
ROSA

Dublin from Irish Independence

Many in Ireland had been pushing towards the restoration of Home Rule during the late nineteenth and early twentieth century without success. During the early years of the twentieth century, the plight of the poor rural Irish farmer and the squalid conditions of Dublin's inner city, combined with an idealized Gaelic revival movement, had rekindled home rule and independence movements. Growing civic unrest and tension, such as the great tram strike of 1913, were preludes to more significant disturbances.

The tide of discontent reached a major flash point in 1916, when on Easter Monday a group of fiercely idealistic patriots, led by popular Irish trade unionist James Connolly and poet Patrick Pearse, inspired an uprising in Dublin they hoped would lead to a greater revolution and ultimately Irish independence. They seized a number of strategic buildings in Dublin, among them the recently restored General Post Office where Pearse read aloud a carefully prepared Proclamation of Independence. As in the past, response to rebellion was swift and harsh. Despite distractions of the First World War, a British gunship was sent up the Liffey where it shelled rebel strongholds. Thousands of British troops poured into Dublin from the dozen army garrisons across the city. Fighting raged for six days before the Rising was crushed and its leaders arrested.

The Rising has been of special interest to Dubliners, not just because it was the spark that led to Irish independence, but because the key battles were fought on Dublin's streets. Furthermore, many of its principal participants, if not celebrities before the Rising, have since been enshrined in both Dublin and Irish lore. Yet, initially, many Dubliners were horrified by the Rising and the destruction to their city. The GPO was a smoldering ruin with bricks and rubble strewn across main streets. What turned the tide of Irish opinion was the execution of 15 of the Rising leaders. Most were shot at Kilmainham Gaol, including the gravely wounded Connolly who was tied to a chair. Although the Rising had been unpopular, many of its leaders had been popular figures. Their executions had made them martyrs. Connolly, for one, had a great public following and was well liked among the working class; word of his death sparked outrage.

Public response to the Easter Rising was delayed, following the General Election of 1918 when many Nationalists were elected to government. Tensions worsened and a bloody war between Ireland and Britain resulted. To better understand this Anglo-Irish conflict, it should be placed in the larger European context. It was an age of new-found nationalism and idealistic revolution largely fueled by same undercurrents that had resulted in the First World War (sparked by the actions of Serbian nationalists in Sarajevo). Nationalist movements occurred concurrently in a variety of European countries. Most significant was the Russian Revolution which led to creation of the Soviet Union. In Ireland, the initial conflict raged for two years. In 1921, a settlement was offered resulting in partition of the country creating the

PREVIOUS PAGE: One of the main entrances to St. Stephen's Green is the Fusilier's Arch that commemorates Irish soldiers who died in the Boer War. Beyond is the multistorey Stephen's Green Shopping Centre, built in 1989.

RIGHT: Such a common sight: traffic in Dublin's streets on a damp spring evening. The junction of main streets, Kelly's Corner on the city's south side has been the regular site of tailbacks since the advent of the "Celtic Tiger".

Irish Free State, consisting of 26 southern counties including Dublin. Although the settlement was accepted by one faction of Irish nationalists, the partition produced a new controversial political divide that spurred a vicious Irish Civil War between pro- and anti-partition factions. By 1923, a truce between these factions allowed the Irish Free State to come into being, yet some of the root issues have never been resolved and remain controversial.

The structural effects on Dublin from the wars and the creation of the Free State were multifaceted. Many prominent buildings in the city had been ruined as a result of fighting. Among these were the iconic structures of the GPO, Custom House and the Four Courts. The crucial change was that Dublin again became the seat of Nationalist government. A new Irish Parliament was formed with Leinster House, located off Merrion Square, established as the new Parliament building. Over ensuing decades many place names were changed: Kingstown reverted to its traditional "Dún Laoghaire", Sackville Street (renamed in the 1880s) was officially accepted as O'Connell Street, and so on.

Independent Ireland was driven by idealistic, cultural, and economic desires, not all of which were either satisfied or immediately addressed by creation of the Free State. Name changes put a new spin on old buildings, while the adoption of the Irish language as the official language of state undoubtedly pleased many in their quest to promote Gaelic cultural values. Yet basic economic problems continued to plague Ireland. Its economy, despite political and cultural separation, was inexorably linked to Britain. While a new sympathetic Irish government could address some of the inequities of previous administrations, pro-Irish actions sometimes exacerbated the country's weak economic position in the early years of independence. Dublin continued to suffer from many of the same problems that it had had since Victorian times, and development was stagnant for decades.

The Republic of Ireland was declared in 1949 which further separated the 26 southern counties from Britain. The troubles in the six counties of Northern Ireland are legendary and an often told story in the news; the details of that plight do not need repeating here. However, from the mid-1960s until the 1990s, the troubles in Northern Ireland would affect Dublin in many ways.

Tight national purse strings in Ireland for much of the twentieth century essentially placed Dublin city center in something of a time warp (although the buildings damaged during the struggle for independence were either faithfully restored or demolished). The city had taken its bruises during the fight for independence and, though Ireland remained neutral in the First World War, it nevertheless underwent a German bombing raid. However, it had not suffered the fate of many European cities leveled due to extensive bombing and street fighting. While Dublin had lost a few buildings, casualties among its residents were relatively few, and the city was largely intact.

Furthermore, while there was some new construction in central Dublin between the 1950s and the 1980s, it was not subject to the widespread urban renewal that changed the look and character of so many other cities in this period. True, a few dual carriageways were carved here and there, but the city largely avoided the urban chaos caused by cutting major highways through its heart. The basic layout of central Dublin would be familiar to James Joyce if he were to walk the city today. Unfortunately, the few large buildings that have been constructed seem to have embraced the same starvation level planning that gripped the country during its lean years.

Structures such as Liberty Hall (a trade union office), the Electrical Supply Board's offices on Lower Fitzwilliam Street and the monstrosity known as O'Connell Bridge House are out of character and out of scale with the Georgian city that surrounds them. More imposing are

Left: O'Connell Street is Dublin's widest thoroughfare; central to the street is the Spire, installed in 2002-03. On the right is the General Post Office, built in 1818, destroyed in 1916 and restored in the 1920s.

two major buildings designed by Sam Stephenson and Associates—the new Central Bank on Dame Street, and the new Dublin Corporation offices on Wood Quay—that stand out because of their modern design. The latter proved exceptionally controversial, not only as a result of its architectural styling but because a 1,000-year old Viking settlement was unearthed during its construction and then quickly destroyed despite mass protests.

Throughout the twentieth century, Dublin tended to grow out rather than up, with most development occurring in the suburbs as new housing estates as communities were built to house the city's increasing population. Many attractive new houses have been built by Dublin's expanding middle class. Government efforts at dealing with Dublin's infamous slums resulted in relocating people to modern public housing in and beyond the city. As with efforts in other countries aimed at solving social inequity through state planning, Dublin's produced mixed results. Overcrowding may have been alleviated, but other problems associated with poverty were simply shifted from one place to another. The tower block housing at Ballymun is the best known of Dublin's state-of-the-art slums, immortalized by a U2 song in the 1980s.

New roads have been built, and new routes planned and conceived. Several significant segments of motorway were in place by the mid-1990s, including the beginnings of an orbital highway known as the M50. In the sphere of public transport, Ireland made nominal investments in its railways. Many lines were closed between the 1950s and 1970s—including Dublin's Harcourt Street Line. Ireland was, however, the first country in western Europe to import U.S. General Motors-built diesel locomotives, and the first European nation to completely end the operation of steam locomotives, except for the Railway Preservation Society of Ireland's historic excursions. In the early 1980s, Dublin made the move to electrify its busiest suburban rail routes, including the old D&KR line, and branded the new electric trains as Dublin Area Rapid Transit, or "DART".

LEFT: The traditional session is an old feature of Dublin's pubs. In recent years, tourists rather than locals tend to seek out the music.

RIGHT: The Wide Streets Commission could not have anticipated twentieth century transport needs. Today's traffic may be headed further afoot than Gardiner Square…Er… sorry, Mountjoy Square.

N1
Béal Feirste
BELFAST
Aerphort

LEFT: Too often abandoned buildings meet their end through fire. The Dublin Fire Brigade attends to a blaze at Kelly's Corner in summer 2000.

RIGHT: Yesterday's fire may be tomorrow's building site. Firemen contain the flames at an abandoned house at Kelly's Corner. Smoke could be smelled from a half mile away. The Dublin Fire Brigade was formed in 1862.

FOLLOWING PAGE: Dublin's port facilities were greatly expanded in the 1960s. To the rightlled, note Electrical Supply Board's Pool Beg Generating Station built on reclaimed land in the twentieth century. Its stacks are the highest structures in Dublin.

DUBLIN FIRE BRIGADE
telephone
television
As nature intended.
SPAR
DENNIS
GB Fire
97-D-57009
Sabre
BURNS
WASTE
BURNS
WASTE

CAF
HARNS

www.IrishJobs.ie
Where do you see yourself?
music epicentre
Dublin Bus

LEFT: Dublin installed its first horse tram line in 1872; electric trams operated beginning in 1896 and were a significant feature of Joycean Dublin. The last traditional city trams ended in 1949 although many Dublin bus routes, such as the No. 19 seen here on Harrington Street, still follow the old tram routes.

FOLLOWING PAGE: Kingsbridge was installed in 1828 to commemorate King George IV's 1821 visit to Dublin; it was renamed Sean Heuston Bridge in 1941. At the time of this 1999 photo, the bridge was a rusty tired relic of an earlier age.

KINGSBRIDGE

PREVIOUS PAGE: Sean Heuston Bridge following renovation and strengthening to handle modern LUAS trams. Lit up to the left, Heuston Station was renamed in 1966 for the hero of the Easter Rising.

LEFT: Redevelopment of Temple Bar and vicinity in the 1990s was a major boost to the artistic and commercial life of Dublin's city center.

RIGHT: The imposing structure of the Central Bank—suspended from the top and built from top to bottom—is a contrast to the Georgian and Victorian buildings around it.

WOOLLEN MILLS TRIMMINGS
Ha'penny Bridge Inn

PREVIOUS PAGE: By the late 1990s, Dublin's old cast iron Liffey Bridge was in need of an overhaul. During much of 2000-01 the bridge was closed and totally renovated. It is now painted light beige rather than silver.

LEFT: The sorry condition of many of Dublin's finest Georgian buildings in the twentieth century characterized Ireland's economic woes.

RIGHT AND BELOW: Trade union leader Jim Larkin roused the crowds on O'Connell Street in 1913. A statue commemorating his speech stands across from Clery's Department Store.

LEFT: Symbols of Irish independence: the Tri-Color snaps in the wind over the General Post Office on O'Connell Street. On the left is the statue of Fidelity, to the right, Hibernia is at ease with spear in hand.

RIGHT: The Four Courts, Ireland's High Court, is a regular feature in Ireland's news.

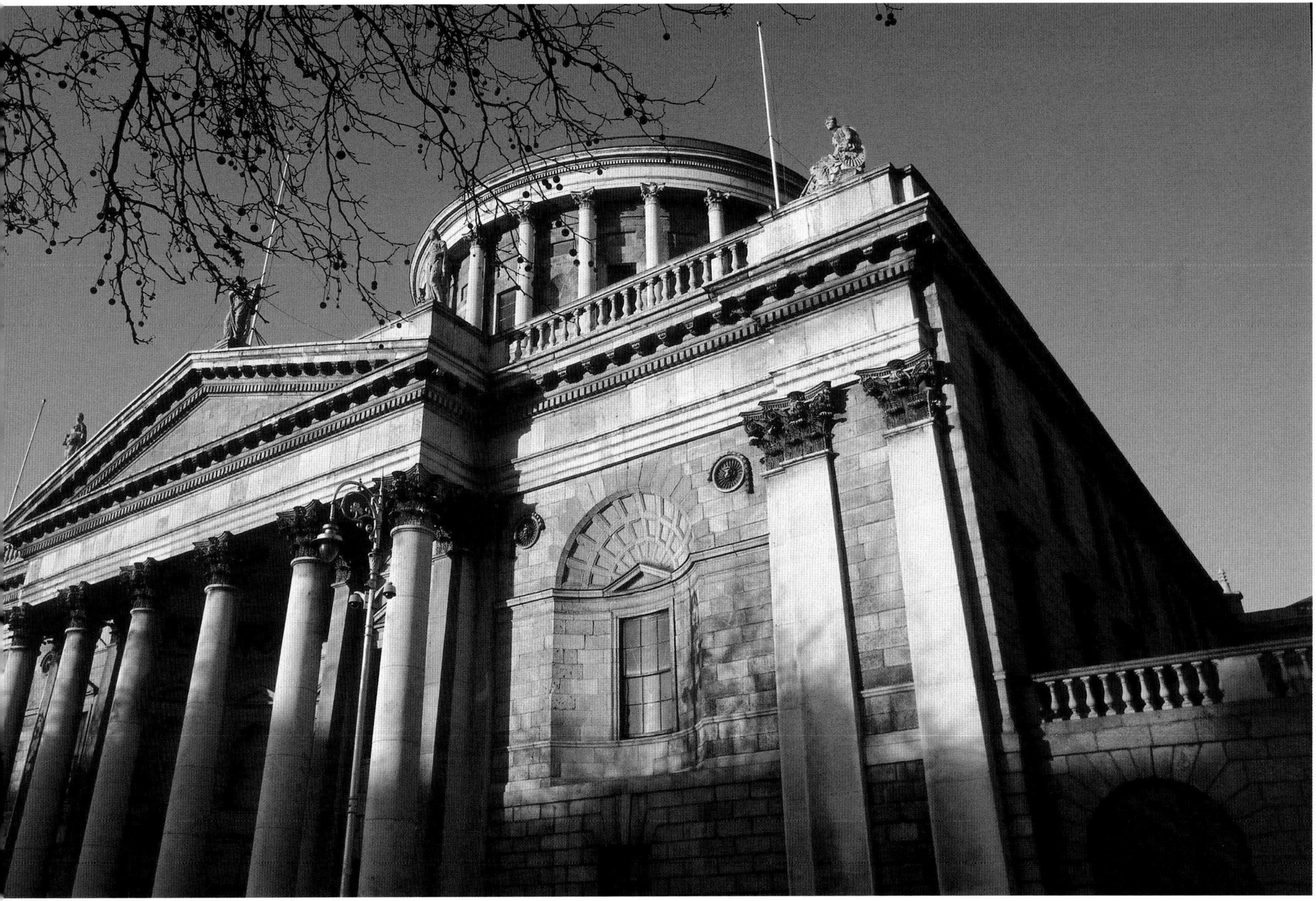

SAORSTÁT ÉIREANN

Left: A harp facing the River Liffey adorns the Four Courts.

Right: Among Dublin's prominent brew pubs is this fine establishment on Burgh Quay opposite the O'Connell Bridge.

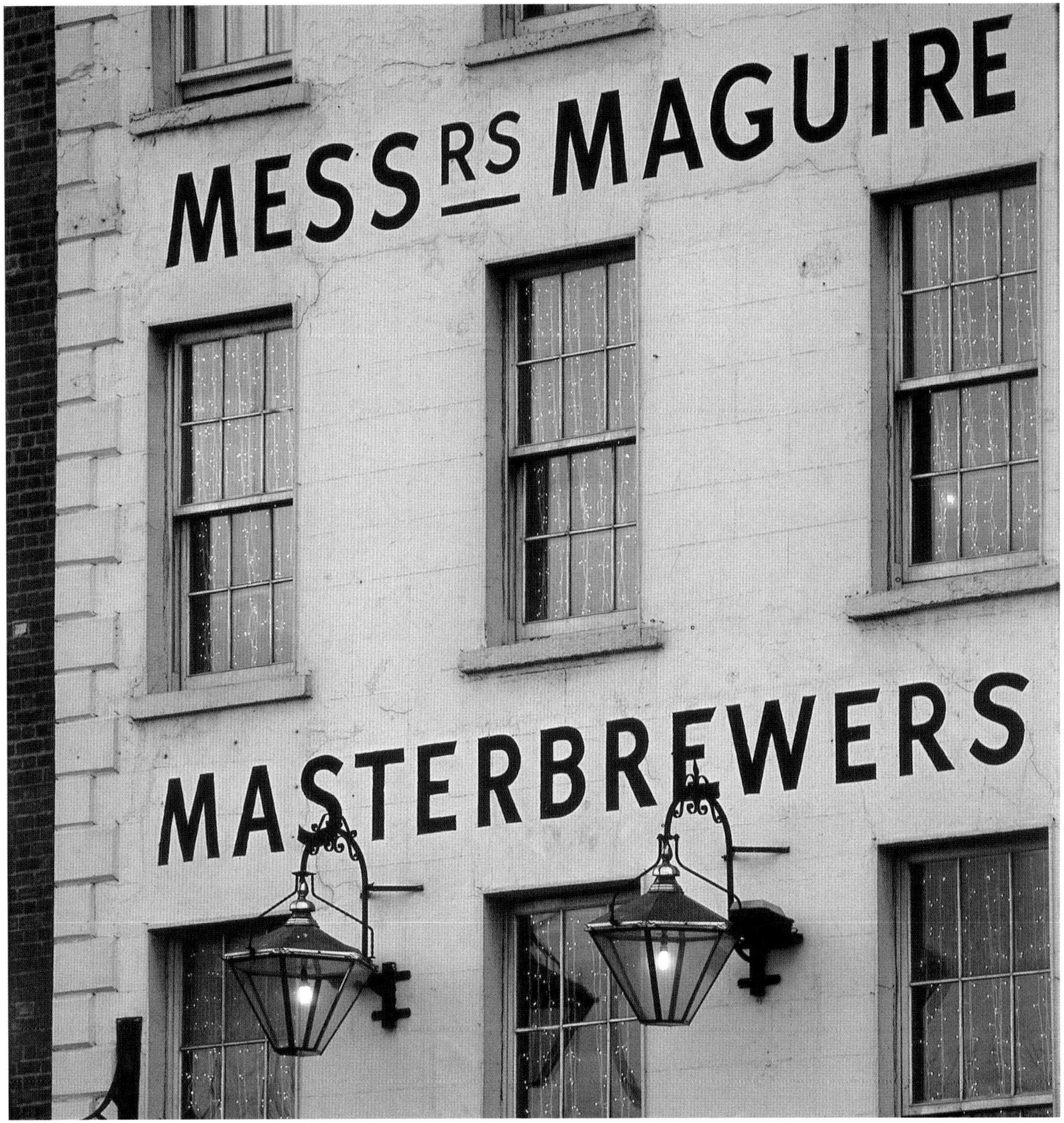

FACE JACKS
CLUB

LEFT: Harcourt Street's Georgian splendor transcends the gloom of a damp evening. Since this 1990s view, tracks for the LUAS have been added to the street.

RIGHT: The cobbles at Temple Bar catch the glint of the evening sun.

LEFT: John Henry Foley's 1882 O'Connell Monument contrasts with the spartan 1960s architecture of the O'Connell Bridge House across the Liffey.

RIGHT: Charles Steward Parnell led the movement for Home Rule in the mid-nineteenth century. He is commemorated at the north end of O'Connell Street.

FAR RIGHT: The Parnell Monument features his most remembered proclamation.

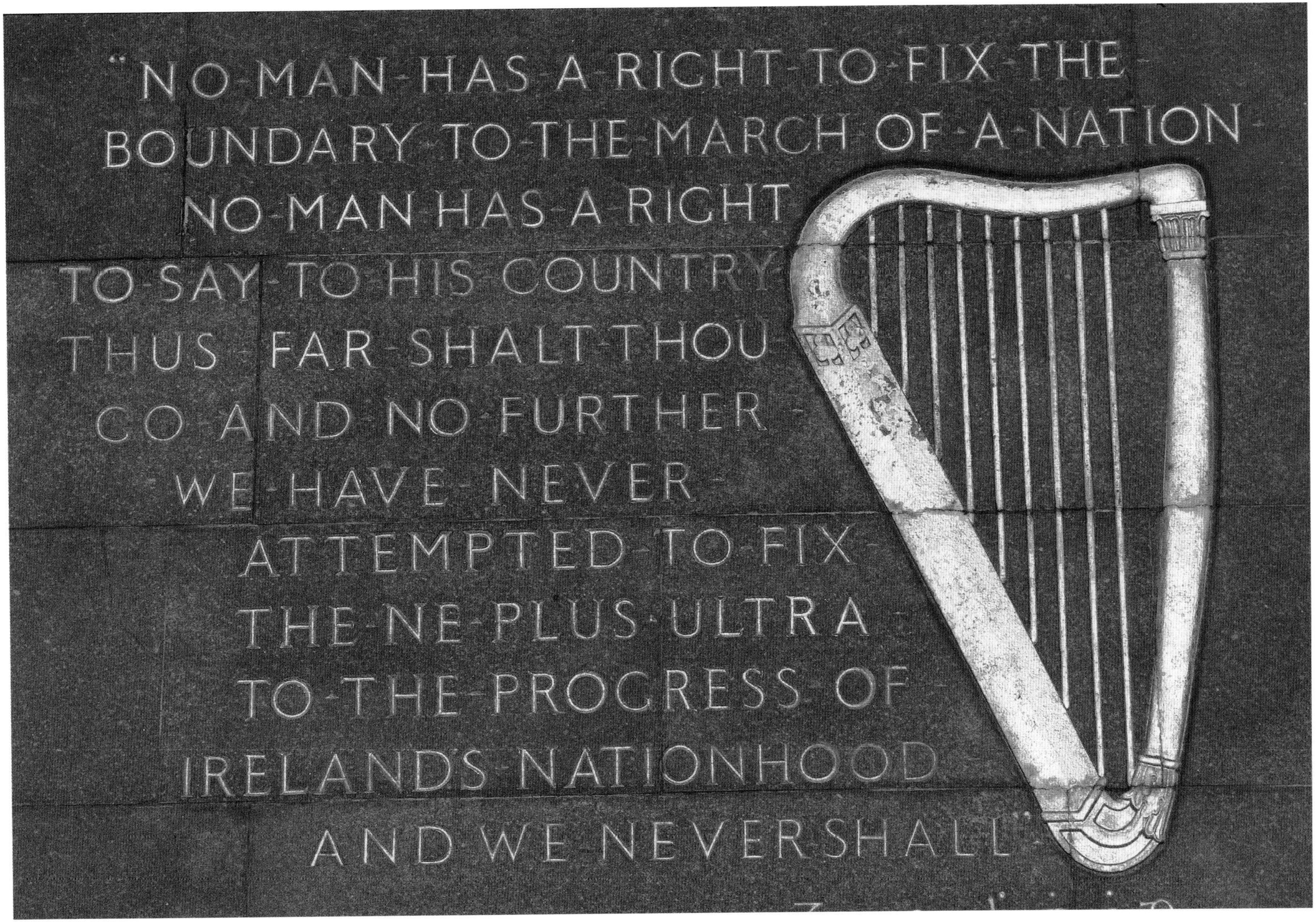
"NO-MAN-HAS-A-RIGHT-TO-FIX-THE
BOUNDARY-TO-THE-MARCH-OF-A-NATION
NO-MAN-HAS-A-RIGHT
TO-SAY-TO-HIS-COUNTRY
THUS-FAR-SHALT-THOU
GO-AND-NO-FURTHER
WE-HAVE-NEVER
ATTEMPTED-TO-FIX
THE-NE-PLUS-ULTRA
TO-THE-PROGRESS-OF
IRELANDS-NATIONHOOD
AND-WE-NEVER-SHALL"

Left: The Government Buildings off Merrion Street Upper were built as the Royal College of Science in the early years of the twentieth century. Today these house ministerial offices and the office of "An Taoiseach"—the Prime Minister.

Right: A city in transition: in the early years of the twenty-first century new buildings rise from the ashes of the old as youth enjoy the vibe of the "Celtic Tiger".

Right: Traffic was light at Mountjoy Square on this March 2000 afternoon.

SRÁID MAC GLOBÚIN
FITZGIBBON STREET
1

IN YOUR ELEMENT
GUINNESS
GUINNESS
GUINNESS

Left: Enjoying pints at Fallon's pub on Dean Street.

Right: The 1990s saw rapid economic turn around, yet evidence of decay was still prevalent in many parts of Dublin.

RIGHT: Vacant lots and disused property along Dean Street waiting for someone with vision and the right price.

Professional
PAINT
STRIPPING
Service
The Old Coombe
FURNITURE & CURIOS
TEL. 4530945
ANTIQUES
BOUGHT
& SOLD
NO PARKING
THE SNUG
PUB ARTEFACTS
& BRIC-A-BRAC
PUB DISPLAY
PAINT STRIPPING SERVICE
J J FAGAN
OPEN

ERCRUGBY.COM
Heineken

LEFT: One of the great rugby venues, Lansdowne Road saw many a battle—here Perpignan and Toulouse fight for the Heineken Cup in 2003. Currently it is under renovation. *Getty Images*

RIGHT: While Lansdowne Road is being developed, Croagh Park—seat of the Gaelic Athletic Association, is being used for rugby and soccer games. This is a 2007 general view of the stadium. *David Rogers/Getty Images*

STOKES

Far left: The Irish Tri-Color snaps in the wind in front of the Custom House. Gandon's masterpiece was cleaned and renovated in the 1990s.

Left: Cantilevered boardwalks were erected along the Liffey's north quays in the city center as part of Dublin's Millennium celebrations. Seagulls scream and soar as they follow the evening tide upriver.

LEFT: Dublin's first planned Georgian neighborhood at Henrietta Street has remained in a state of decay despite a flourishing economy.

RIGHT: The magnificent O'Connell Monument facing the O'Connell Bridge was cleaned and renovated in recent years. It gets a mention from Joyce, and has long been a popular meeting place in the city center.

FAR RIGHT: Less well known than the St. Stephen's Green or Phoenix Park, the National War Memorial Garden is a beautifully manicured, classically adorned open space west of the city center. It honors Irish lost in the First and Second World Wars.

Modern Dublin

Carpark Paypoint
Carpark
P

Modern Dublin

Today, Dublin is a hive of activity; the city center is alive with pedestrians and clogged with private automobiles, taxis and buses. It seems that everywhere one looks there is construction. Skeletal cranes loom above the skyline and the sound of drilling is everywhere. Ever taller glass-encased buildings are underway. The commercial districts on Grafton Street, Henry Street, O'Connell Street are so thronged with people in peak hours it can be difficult to navigate. Dublin—which had suffered from neglect and economic frugality for so long—saw a dramatic turnaround in the 1990s. The "Celtic Tiger" economic boom has fueled a dynamic, cosmopolitan whirlwind that transformed the city within a remarkably short span of time.

A variety of changes spurred this transformation. In the 1970s, Ireland joined the European Economic Community, now the European Union. The coalescing of Europe allowed for a high level of investment previously unattainable in Ireland. This, combined with growing globalization and the propensity of American companies to locate offices and facilities outside the United States, favored Ireland and greatly benefited Dublin. Ireland's advantageous tax laws, comparatively streamlined bureaucracy and highly educated, English-speaking population made Ireland—especially Dublin—ideal for many American businesses. Irish tourism, vigorously promoted in the lean years, has also had an important role. Dublin has long been marketed as a culturally intensive, literary and fun destination. It has been a popular landing point for Americans with Irish roots to learn and rediscover their heritage. And it has been a golfer's paradise.

In recent years there has been a greater focus on European tourists as well as business travelers. Dublin's vibrant pub culture, its well-established literary history, combined with development of areas such as Temple Bar in the city center and the perceived friendliness and humor of its residents have all helped make it a desirable destination for weekend, week-long and, in some cases, life-long visitors. A crucial contribution to Dublin and Ireland's tourism in recent years has been the development and expansion of Dublin Airport and the advent of low-cost airlines such as Ryanair. Where Ireland's island-status once resulted in comparative isolation towards the rest of Europe, Dublin is now little more than a couple of hours away from dozens of major and minor cities across the continent. Dublin and London have more flights between them than any other city pairing in Europe.

In the last decade, the flood of public and private investment has transformed Dublin and its city center. In addition to rabid urban growth in the form of new construction, many older buildings have been revitalized, recycled or otherwise altered. Although it's still possible to find elements of the decay that characterized the Dublin of decades past—even now one can see abandoned buildings with trees growing out of them, and ruined walls standing forlornly in vacant lots can been viewed in the city center—the "Dirty Old Town" has an evermore modern gloss over its Georgian layout.

Among the recent additions to the city center are the ultramodern LUAS tram lines, opened in 2004. Unlike the acronym DART, "Luas" is an Irish word translated as "speed" in English. To the casual observer, the svelte Alstom-built LUAS trams may not seem so speedy, but by using sophisticated priority signaling, and running outside the city center on a largely separate alignment, LUAS transit times are much quicker than road transport. Since opening, LUAS not only captured a good portion of traffic moving along its two routes, but in fact created its own market by providing a convenient, fast and, most of all, reliable service. The LUAS Green Line, which terminates at the Stephen's Green, utilized much of the long abandoned Harcourt Street railway line.

LUAS has been one good aspect of Dublin's transport infrastructure which has largely bogged down because of rapid growth. Despite improvements such as LUAS, Ireland's growing dependence on highways has resulted in furthering the modal shift away from railways, most notably in the province of freight transport. However, in the last few years, higher investment in Irish Rail has produced great improvements to both suburban and long distance passenger services along with the restoration of main railway terminals, the opening of new suburban stations, and extensions of DART electrification. Railway ridership is at an all time high, even if market share has sagged. A number of further key rail infrastructure improvements are on the horizon.

Among significant improvements to Dublin's highway network is the Port Tunnel which opened in 2006, resulting in redirection for most truck traffic away from city center quays to orbital routes. Until the tunnel opened, the quays were typically clogged with

PREVIOUS PAGE: September 2006 finds concrete columns being erected along St. John's Road West opposite Heuston Station for the new Eircom building.

RIGHT: Gaelic Athletic Association's premier sporting venue at Croagh Park received a major renovation and substantial expansion in recent years.

Gill's
GUINNESS
INTERTOOL
JAMES GILL

international lorries navigating the city center to reach the port. What few Dubliners have realized is that the new Port Tunnel is really a re-invention of an older concept: around the north side of Dublin exists a Victorian orbital railway route, complete with a long tunnel beneath Phoenix Park. This had seen declining use largely as the result of the Government's pro-highway freight transport policies.

Even the role and location of Dublin port has come into question in recent years, with some advocating the relocation of the primary port functions well north of the city. Part of the impetus for this notion seems to have been the rapid redevelopment of property by the Docklands Authority east of the city center. Land once occupied by railway freight yards, canal docks, gas works, warehouses, and shipping concerns have become sites of ever-expanding modern office complexes, condominiums and, in the case of the old Point Depot, a popular entertainment venue. Glass-encased high-rises look more like developments found in southern California than anything one would expect to see in Ireland. Here, old James Joyce would stand astonished, and even modern-day locals find the changes difficult to comprehend.

Among notable recent additions in the city center is the Millennium Walkway that resembles pedestrian-friendly open mall architecture characteristic of modern developments in London. This features a number of trendy wine bars, restaurants and cafes, and a wall adorned with a contemporary adaptation of Leonardo's "Last Supper". Located between Abbey Street (opposite the Jervis Center) and Ormond Quay, the Millennium Walkway directs pedestrians across the Liffey via the Millennium footbridge which opened in 2000, and provides easy access to the cobblestone alleyways and eclectic environs of Temple Bar. Further up the Liffey,

LEFT: Old pubs are gradually giving way to new more modern buildings. The new Nash's Pub on the corner of Patrick and Kevin Streets sits on the same site as the old pub of the same name.

beyond the Four Courts, is another modern bridge, named for none other than James Joyce. This very modern-looking, 40-meter span uses parabolic arch supports to suspend the roadway and adjacent footpaths on 32 pairs of steel hangers. In the docklands, the modern Sean O'Casey footbridge is suspended across the river, and the Samuel Beckett highway bridge is expected to open in 2010. In recent years, O'Connell Street—Dublin's main north-south thoroughfare—has been revitalized and improved. In addition to a general clean up, Dubliners saw the notable installation of a monumental stainless steel spire situated on the location once occupied by Nelson's Pillar. The Pillar was perceived as an aesthetic element that tied the layout of the street together. It had suffered sudden, unsanctioned removal in 1966. The Spire, completed in January 2003, is a fascinating piece of artwork that can be observed from a great distance because of its exceptional height—120 meters. (Only the stacks of ESB's Poolbeg Generating Station are taller. These icons, erected between 1969 and 1978, measure 207 meters high.)

Economic prosperity has flooded Dublin with immigrants, resulting in a host of new and evermore diverse eateries, and has attracted a wider range of commercial goods in the shops. In the old days, eating out may have been limited to a trip to the pub for Irish Stew or Shepherd's Pie, or to the local "Chipper" for fish and chips, but today there seems to be no end of international cuisine on offer. Dublin hosts several up-market Sushi bars and a good variety of Indian, Mediterranean, Middle-Eastern, and Chinese restaurants. The other side of Dublin's commercialization has been the loss of a great many traditional shops, pubs and venues as high-volume chains, modern mega-pubs and expensive trendy clubs have moved in. The rise of the

Right: The vitality of Temple Bar has proved an excellent adaptation of the old quayside.

internet saw explosive growth in internet cafes and phone shops during the late 1990s. This was a short-lived boom with the advent of wireless internet (WiFi) and increased home broadband access, so the demand for off-the-street internet cafes has waned dramatically.

The astronomically high cost of commercial rent in Dublin has resulted in a rapid turnaround of shops, restaurants and services. Wandering the streets of Dublin, it seems that businesses come and go on a daily basis. Keeping up with the name changes, or rather failing to keep up, is a notable Dublin trend: "That pub on Wexford Street, the one they call the 'Modern Green', it's been known as 'Solas' since December 2002."

Dublin, which had become a stagnant decaying relic of another era, has been redefined by continual change. To some it is progress, to others it is the force of ruin. In 2007, Dubliners were shocked when a glitch in the economy saw property values dip for the first time in recent memory, yet they yearn for the nostalgic days when a musty, rundown Georgian house could have been purchased for a pittance. Modern Dublin is a city of metamorphosis—every passing day finds something new to look at, or something old to rediscover.

RIGHT: Marks & Spencer's prominent Grafton Street store was the original location of Brown Thomas, now across the street. Christmas window displays reflect the rising affluence of Dublin's middle class.

FAR RIGHT: The largest obelisk in Europe, the Wellington Testimonial catches a blast of sun on a stormy afternoon.

RIGHT: Among the most recent Liffey crossings is the James Joyce Bridge. A pair of angled parabolic arches suspend a roadway deck that spans 40 meters.

INSOMNIA
SPAR
INSOMNIA
SPAR

LEFT: Young leprechauns watch the annual St. Patrick's Day parade cross the O'Connell Bridge.

RIGHT: Everyone gets into the spirit of St. Patrick's Day in Dublin. Dressed for the occasion of the Parade, residents and visitors are poised for a good time at College Green.

BUS

LEFT: St. Patrick's Day has become an annual display of increasingly silly hats.

RIGHT: Flags displaying symbols of Dublin and Ireland fly over Ormond Quay. The three burning castles stem from medieval times symbolizing repeated raids on Dublin from Gaelic-Irish living beyond "the Pale".

LEFT: Students paint faces for charity on Temple Bar on St. Patrick's Day.

Right: The original Carlisle Bridge was designed by James Gandon and named for Dublin's Lord Lieutenant. Significantly widened in 1880, the bridge is now wider than it is long. The name was changed to O'Connell Bridge in the 1920s.

Heineken

RIVER PARK
www.clancyquay.ie
631 8402

LEFT: An artist's vision of redevelopment of the old Clancy Barracks at Islandbridge contrast with the old barrack walls. Blending new architecture with existing buildings in the modern complex will form links with the past.

FOLLOWING PAGE: Patrons gather outside the Millennium as LUAS trams pass on Benburb Street in front of the old Ashling Hotel building—demolished in spring 2008 as part of the hotel's upgrading. The Millennium Bar commemorates Dublin's 1,000 year celebration in 1988, and not the year 2000.

HOTEL
PARKING
BED
&
BREAKFAST

THE MILLENNI
BAR & LOUNGE
THE MILLENNIU
AT ALL TIMES
Wines
Fürstenberg

LEFT: The No. 1 Locks on the Grand Canal at Suir Road on Dublin's south side. LUAS runs parallel to the canal at this point, then continues east in a portion of the old canal bed that once reached St. James Street Harbor.

RIGHT: By December 2007, exterior glass had been installed on the new Eircom building but completion of the modern structure was still several months away.

LEFT: An Aer Lingus Airbus takes off at Dublin Airport for America.

SWAROVSKI
www.dublinbus.ie

Left: Dublin Bus (or "Bus Atha Cliath") provides an intensive public transport service for the greater Dublin area. A courteous tradition: Dubliners thank their driver when leaving the bus.

Right: Dublin icons from left to right: Liberty Hall; the Spire; and the Custom House. In the foreground is the Sean O'Casey footbridge over the Liffey.

Right: Modern office blocks characterize waterfront development by the Docklands Authority. In recent years rapid growth on both sides of the Liffey has completely changed the look of the Docklands.

RIGHT: Fruits of the "Celtic Tiger"; the "new" Dublin is built on reclaimed land previously occupied by waterfront industries.

Forbes Street
Sir John Rogerson's Quay
City Centre

Left: Buildings of glass, steel and concrete at Sir John Rogerson's Quay seem alien in comparison with Georgian Dublin.

Right: Sparkling new residential developments such as Pembroke Square at Grand Canal Docks present a stark contrast with the run down industrial buildings that were prevalent in this area just a decade ago.

CAFFE CAGLIOSTRO
OPEN

LEFT: The Millennium Walkway located between Abbey Street Upper and Ormond Quay features a modern interpretation of Leonardo's "Last Supper".

RIGHT: The LUAS Green Line crosses the Taney Bridge at Dundrum. This modern asymmetrical cable-stayed bridge was designed by Roughan and O'Donovan, the firm that also participated in the design of the James Joyce Bridge over the Liffey.

LEFT: Its motors humming, an Alstom-built Citadis type tram glides down Harcourt Street near the LUAS Green Line terminus at St. Stephen's Green.

RIGHT: A rainy evening on Abbey Street finds a LUAS tram waiting for the lights to cross O'Connell Street. Trams negotiate Abbey Street in the city center.

GOVINDAS
VEGETARIAN
RESTAURANT
00-D-56652

INDA'S

Left: In a blur of fluorescent light and metallic lavender paint, LUAS trams hum past each other at the busy intersection of Abbey and O'Connell Streets.

Right: The O'Connell Monument and the Spire are two of Dublin's most prominent public features. The former was unveiled in 1882, the latter in 2003.

EUROPA

LEFT: Named for Henry Moore, the Earl of Drogheda, Henry Street is a thriving commercial area perpendicular to O'Connell Street.

RIGHT: Ian Ritchie designed Dublin's Spire which rises 120 meters above O'Connell Street, filling the visual roll once played by Nelson's Pillar.

Left: A Christmas morning silhouette of O'Connell Street emphasizes the central location of the Spire.

Inset: The Spire reflects surrounding buildings.
iStockphoto

Left: Normally one of Dublin's busiest streets, Christmas morning finds O'Connell Street devoid of traffic and pedestrians. This photo was taken before the street's 2002 refurbishment that resulted in the removal of most of the trees on the center island.

Right: Dublin's compact city center makes walking the best way to get around. Pedestrians crowd Harcourt Street at rush-hour.

LEFT: These days downtown Dublin has the sleek air of a European city. *iStockphoto*

RIGHT: Long a public common, St. Stephen's Green was established as a park in 1663. After years as a private park it was re-opened to the public in 1880 as a gift from the Guinness heir. Its bucolic landscaping, flowers and ponds, makes it a popular refuge from the trials of urban Dublin.

There ain't no finer Diner
Eddie Rocket's
City Diner
GET
IN
HERE
HOT DOGS · Fries · MALTS
There ain't no
Finer Diner
HARDWARE
ROMA II

LEFT AND RIGHT: Eddie Rocket's is a popular restaurant chain patterned after the classic American diner. Wexford Street is one Dublin's busy commercial lanes and is popular for its vibrant night life.

WINE BAR
TEMPLE BAR
Café Beag
The Little Cafe
Café Beag
HOTDOGS
PIZZA SLICE
ICE CREAM
PIZZA
HOT DOGS
24 hours

Left: Temple Bar pulses with Dublin's cultural life. Nearly demolished to make way for a bus terminal, the old buildings and narrow alleys of the Temple Bar area have been adapted into a significant attraction.

Bibliography

Books

— *The Works of W.B. Yeats.* Ware, Hertfordshire: Wordsworth Editions Ltd, 1994.

Behan, Brendan. *After the Wake.* Dublin: The O'Brien Press, 1981.

Boland, Gerry. *Stroller's Guide to Dublin.* Dublin: Gill & Macmillan Ltd, 1999.

Boller, Alfred P. *Practical Treatise on the Construction of Iron Highway Bridges.* New York: John Wiley & Sons, 1876.

Bowers, Maira. *Dublin City Parks & Gardens.* Dublin: The Lilliput Press, 1999.

Brady, Joseph and Anngret Simms. *Dublin through Space & Time.* Dublin: Four Courts Press Ltd., 2001, 2002.

Clarke, Peter. *The Royal Canal—the Complete Story.* Dublin: ELO Publication, 1992.

Connolly, James. *The Re-Conquest of Ireland.* Dublin and Belfast: New Books Publications, 1983.

Conroy, J. C. *A History of Railways in Ireland.* London: Longmans, Green and Co. Ltd, 1928.

Corcoran, Michael. *Through Streets Broad & Narrow.* Leicester: Midland Publishing, 2000.

Cox, Ronald and Michael Gould. *Civil Engineering Heritage—Ireland.* London: Thomas Telford Publishing, 1998.

Cox, Ronald and Michael Gould. *Ireland Bridges.* Dublin: Wolfhound Press, 2003.

DeCourcy, J.W. *The Liffey in Dublin.* Dublin: Gill & Macmillan, 1996.

Delvin, Polly. *American Express Travel Guide Dublin.* New York: Prentice Hall, 1993.

Duffy, Seán. *Atlas of Irish History.* Dublin: Gill & Macmillan Ltd, 1997.

Gerard-Sharp, Lisa and Tim Perry. *Eye Witness Travel—Ireland.* London: Dorling Kindersley Ltd., 1995, 2008.

Giedion, Sigfried. *Space, Time and Architecture.* 4th Edition. Cambridge: Harvard University Press, 1963.

Gillespie, Michael Patrick. *The Works of James Joyce.* Ware, Hertfordshire: Wordsworth Editions Ltc, 1995.

Gilligan, Henry A. *A History of the Port of Dublin.* Dublin: Gill & Macmillan Ltd, 1988.

Jerrares, A. Norman. *Jonathan Swift—The Selected Poems.* London: Kyle Cathie Ltd, 1981.

Johnson, Paul. *Ireland—A Concise History from the Twelfth Century to the Present Day.* Chicago: Academy Chicago Publishers, 1980.

Judt, Tony. *Postwar—A History of Europe Since 1945.* London: William Heinemann, 2005

Kilfeather, Siobhán. *Dublin—A Cultural History.* Oxford University Press, 2005

Kirby, Richard Shelton, and Laurson, Philip Gustave. *The Early Years of Modern Civil Engineering.* London: Oxford University Press, 1932.

Lawlor, T. Anthony. *Irish Maritime Survey.* Dublin: The Parkside Press Limited, 1945.

Lydon, James. *The Making of Ireland—from Ancient Times to the Present.* London: Routledge, 1998.

Maitiú, Séamas Ó. *Dublin's Suburban Towns 1834-1930.* Dublin: Four Courts Press, 2003.

Manning, Maurice and Moore McDowell. *Electricity Supply in Ireland—The History of the ESB.* Dublin: Gill & Macmillan Ltd, 1984.

Murray, K.A. *Ireland's First Railway.* Dublin: The Irish Railway Record Society, 1981.

O' Farrell, Padraic. *How the Irish Speak English.* Dublin: Mercier Press, 1980, 1993.

Ó Riain, Mícheal. *On the Move—Córas Iompair Éieann 1945-1995.* Dublin: Gill & Macmillan Ltd, 1995.

Ó Siochfhradha. *Foclóir Gaeilge/Béarla — English/Irish.* Dublin: Smurfit Services Ltd. 1996.

Robertson, Ian. Blue Guide—Ireland. London: A&C Black, 1987.

Roth, Leland M. *Understanding Architecture: Its Elements, History and Meaning.* Boulder: Westview Press, 1993.

Simmons, Jack. *Rail 150, The Stockton & Darlington Railway and What Followed.* London: Eyre Methuen, 1975.

Solomon, Brian. *Railway Masterpieces, celebrating the world's greatest trains, stations and feats of engineering.* Iola, Wisconsin: Krause, 2002.

Standage, Tom. *A History of the World in 6 Glasses.* New York: Walker Publishing Company, 2006.

Walsh, Claire. *Archaeological Excavation at Patrick, Nicholas & Winetavern Streets Dublin.* Dublin: Brandon, 1997.

Periodicals

Journal of Bridge Engineering. American Society of Civil Engineers, New York.

Journal of the Irish Railway Record Society, Dublin, Ireland.

Proceedings [of the] Blackrock Society, Blackrock, Ireland.

Index